The P(Retirement in the United Kingdom

10 Secrets for Turning your Leave from Work into an Adventure.

Tips and Suggestions for Fighting Boredom and Discovering New Opportunities in Your Life

by

Lothar Friedmann

© Copyright 2024 by Lothar Friedmann. All rights reserved.

This document is intended to provide accurate and reliable information on the subject matter and subject matter covered. The publication is sold with the understanding that the publisher is under no obligation to provide accounting, regulatory or other professional services. If legal or professional advice is required, a person experienced in the profession should be consulted.

Reproduction, duplication or distribution of this document, whether in electronic or printed form, is not authorized in any way. Recording of this publication is strictly prohibited and storage of this document is only permitted with the written authorization of the publisher. All rights reserved.

The information contained herein is true and consistent, so any liability, in terms of carelessness or otherwise, arising from the use or misuse of the policies, procedures or instructions contained herein is solely the responsibility of the reader. In no event shall the publisher be liable for any recovery, damages or financial loss arising directly or indirectly from the information contained herein.

All copyrights not owned by the publisher belong to the respective authors.

The information contained herein is offered for information purposes only and as such is of general validity. The information is presented without any contractual or warranty commitment.

The trademarks used are without any authorization and their publication does not imply the authorization or endorsement of the trademark owner. All trademarks and brands in this book are for identification purposes only and belong to the owners themselves, who are not associated with this book.

Table of Contents

Chapter 1: Introduction to Retirement Life 7
Welcome to the New Phase of Life 7
Transition from Work to Retirement 9
Leisure Planning 11
Setting New Goals and Priorities 13

Chapter 2: Discovering the UK: Travel and Exploration 17
The Hidden Gems of the United Kingdom 19
Train Journeys to Discover the English Countryside 21
Coastal Routes: Beaches and Cliffs 23
Historical Trips: Castles, Abbeys and Monuments 25
Exploring lesser-known locations 27
Themed trips, such as literary trails inspired by famous British authors 34

Chapter 3 Recreational Activities and Hobbies 37
Gardening: From Garden Design to Practical Advice 38
Cooking and Pastry: Traditional and Innovative Recipes 41
Handicrafts: Knitting, Sewing and Crafts 43
Photography and Painting: Expressing Creativity 45

Chapter 4 Sport and Well-being 49
Walking and Hiking: Trails and National Parks 51
Golf: The Best Courses in the UK 52
Water Activities: Boating, Fishing and Sailing 55
Yoga and Meditation: Physical and Mental Wellbeing 57
Introduction to birdwatching and nature reserves in the UK 59
Birdwatching Equipment: My Personal Guide 61
Benefits of forest walks and suggested routes 63

Chapter 5 Volunteering Opportunities 67
Contributing to the Community: Organisations and Associations 69

    Volunteering in Hospitals and Nursing Homes 71

    Environmental and Conservation Projects 74

Chapter 6 Continuous Learning 77

    Online Courses and Universities of the Third Age 79

    Reading and Discussion Clubs 81

    Museums and Galleries: Subscriptions and Guided Tours 83

    Participate in British history or genealogy courses to discover your roots 85

    Lessons in foreign languages or music to stimulate the mind 90

Chapter 7 Social and Group Activities 93

    Clubs and Societies: Joining Groups with Common Interests 95

    Local Events and Fairs 97

    List of Local Events and Fairs 100

    Organise and Participate in Group Excursions 102

Chapter 8 Luxury Travel and Unique Experiences 105

    Luxury Cruises: The Best Offers 106

    Stays in Historic Hotels and Resorts 109

    Gourmet Experiences: Gastronomic Tours and Tastings 111

    Adventure Travel: Safari and Exploration in the UK 113

Chapter 9 Exploring Local Culture 117

    UK Festivals and Cultural Events 119

    Local Markets and Craft Fairs 121

    Theatres, Concerts and Performances 123

    Discovering Local Cuisine: Cookery Courses and Gastronomic Tours 126

    Attend traditional celebrations such as Guy Fawkes Night and the Notting Hill Carnival 128

    Visits to historic breweries and distilleries with tastings of local products .. 130

Chapter 10 Time Management and Emotional Well-being 133

    Balancing Activity and Rest 134

    Maintaining Social and Family Relationships 136

Mindfulness and Relaxation Techniques 138
Solving Common Problems: Loneliness and Mental Health 141
Conclusion: Embracing an Active and Satisfying Retirement 145

ON THE LAST PAGE YOU WILL FIND THE

Chapter 1: Introduction to Retirement Life

Welcome to the New Phase of Life

Retirement represents a completely new chapter in a person's life, a time of transition that can bring with it a mix of emotions, from joy to uncertainty. For many, leaving work means saying goodbye to an established routine, long-standing colleagues and a significant part of one's identity. However, retirement also offers a wonderful opportunity to explore new passions, devote time to neglected interests and build a full and fulfilling life. Here are some key points for how best to embrace this new phase of life.

<u>Reflection and Planning</u>

The first step is reflection. Taking time to reflect on your career, achievements and experiences can help you close this chapter with gratitude and serenity. It is also helpful to plan how you want to spend your free time. Careful planning can make the difference between a retirement full of opportunities and one that may seem empty and directionless.

<u>Set New Goals</u>

Retirement does not mean to stop having goals. On the contrary, it is the ideal time to set new goals. These can include health and fitness goals, such as participating in a marathon or simply maintaining an active lifestyle; educational goals, such as learning a new language or signing up for courses of interest; and social goals, such as volunteering or joining new clubs.

<u>Exploring New Passions and Hobbies</u>

Retirement is the ideal time to pursue interests and pastimes you may have put on hold during your working years because you will have more free time. Gardening, painting, photography, gourmet cooking, and many other hobbies can offer immense satisfaction. In addition, pursuing new interests can help keep the mind active and stimulated, reducing the risk of isolation and depression.

Socializing and Community

One of the most important aspects of retirement is maintaining strong ties to the community and social relationships. Participating in interest groups, clubs, or volunteer organizations can not only fill time but also create a sense of belonging and fulfilment. Local communities offer a wide range of activities that can help build new friendships and strengthen existing ones.

Travelling and discovering the UK

The boarding house offers the opportunity to travel and discover the wonders of the UK. From train journeys through picturesque countryside, to visits to historic castles, spectacular coastlines and charming villages, the UK is full of fascinating destinations. Even the lesser-known locations can offer unique and memorable experiences, allowing you to discover the less touristy side of the country.

Time Management and Emotional Wellbeing

With the freedom to have your own time, it is important to balance activity and rest. Establishing a flexible but structured routine can help give a sense of normalcy and purpose to the day. In addition, practicing mindfulness and meditation techniques can help maintain emotional well-being, reducing stress and promoting a positive outlook on life.

Facing Challenges

Finally, it is natural to face some challenges during the transition to retirement. Managing finances, health and sense of identity can be areas of concern. It is helpful to seek support when needed, be it financial counselling, support groups or mental health professionals. Meeting these challenges with proactivity and resilience can make retirement an extremely rewarding and fulfilling time.

In conclusion, retirement is a phase of life full of potential and opportunity. Embracing this transition with a positive and open attitude can lead to discovering new passions, building meaningful relationships and living a full and fulfilling life. Welcome to your new adventure!

Transition from Work to Retirement

A person's move from the workforce to retirement is a crucial and frequently difficult time in their life. After decades of working routine, moving on to a phase of freedom and leisure can be both exciting and disorienting. Here are some crucial aspects to best manage this transition, ensuring a fulfilling and peaceful retirement.

<u>Mental and Emotional Preparation</u>

It is imperative that you first mentally and emotionally get ready for the change. In addition to providing money, work is essential to one's social and personal identity. Retirement can therefore bring with it a sense of loss of purpose. Dealing with these emotions is essential. Talking about it with friends, family or a counsellor can help to process these feelings. Also, visualizing retirement as an opportunity rather than an end can help maintain a positive attitude.

<u>Financial planning</u>

Careful financial planning is crucial for a stress-free transition. Before retiring, it is advisable to consult a financial advisor to assess your resources and ensure that your savings and pensions are sufficient to maintain your desired lifestyle. Understanding how state and private pensions work, and knowing about possible tax benefits, can make a big difference. It is also helpful to create a budget that considers both current expenses and any unexpected costs.

<u>Establish a New Routine</u>

One of the biggest challenges of retirement is the lack of a daily structure. Creating a new routine can help give meaning and purpose to your days. This can include activities such as exercise, hobbies, volunteering or participation in social groups. Having a routine does not mean filling every minute of the day, but rather creating a balance between activity and time for rest.

Developing New Passions and Interests

Retirement provides the chance to pursue interests and passions that were overlooked during the working years. Whether it is learning a new language, taking up painting, or cultivating a garden, engaging in new activities can be extremely rewarding. Taking part in local or online courses can also be a great way to acquire new skills and meet people with similar interests.

Maintaining Social Relationships

Work often provides a social network that can be lacking once you retire. It is important to maintain and build new social relationships. Participating in clubs, voluntary organizations, or common interest groups can help you stay connected and prevent social isolation. Social relationships are crucial for emotional and mental well-being.

Taking Care of Physical and Mental Health

Health must remain a priority. Continuing to exercise regularly, eating a balanced diet and maintaining routine medical check-ups are all essential practices. Mental health is also important: practices such as meditation, mindfulness, and reading can help keep the mind active and healthy. Participating in activities that stimulate the brain, such as board games, puzzles or continuous learning, can help maintain mental clarity.

Embrace Change with Flexibility

Finally, embracing change with flexibility is crucial. Retirement is a dynamic and evolving phase. It is normal for plans to change and priorities to shift over time. Adopting a flexible attitude and being open to new experiences can make the transition much more enjoyable and less stressful.

In conclusion, the transition from work to retirement is a time of great change, but with the right preparation and mindset, it can turn into one of life's most fulfilling periods. Accepting and adapting to this new phase with positivity and proactivity can open the door to new adventures and discoveries.

Leisure Planning

Retirement represents a unique opportunity to redefine how one spends one's time. After years of working routines, having the freedom to manage your own time can be both exciting and intimidating. Effective leisure planning is essential to ensure an active, rewarding and purposeful life. Here are some crucial aspects to consider to better plan your free time in retirement.

Identifying Passions and Interests

The first step in planning your free time is to identify your passions and interests. Reflecting on what you love to do can help you define which activities to include in your daily routine. Whether gardening, reading, painting, cooking, or sports, it is important to choose activities that bring joy and satisfaction. Also consider activities that you wanted to try but never had time to explore during your working years.

Create a Flexible Routine

Having a routine, even a flexible one, can help give structure to your days. A routine does not have to be rigid but can include regular activities such as exercise in the morning, reading in the afternoon and social activities or hobbies in the evening. Having a routine helps maintain a sense of purpose and discipline, preventing boredom and inactivity. It is also important to include times of rest and relaxation to avoid burnout.

Participate in Social Activities

Socializing is a key element of a happy and fulfilling retirement. Participating in clubs, interest groups, or voluntary organizations can help maintain a strong connection to the community. Social activities not only fill time but also offer opportunities to create new friendships and strengthen existing relationships. Consider joining reading groups, gardening clubs, art classes, or participating in local events.

Experience New Adventures

Retirement is an ideal time to experience new adventures and step out of your comfort zone. Travelling, both locally and abroad, can offer enriching and memorable experiences. Discovering new cultures, landscapes and traditions can be extremely rewarding. Planning trips to lesser-known locations in the UK, such as the coastal villages of Northumberland or the countryside of Wales, can offer unique experiences away from the more crowded tourist destinations.

Learn and Grow

The desire to learn should never fade. Retirement offers time to acquire new skills and knowledge. Enrolling in online courses or at local universities, attending seminars, or taking classes on topics of interest can be very stimulating. Learning new languages, musical instruments, or artistic techniques are just some of the endless possibilities available.

Taking care of your health

Maintaining an active lifestyle is essential to fully enjoy free time. Regular physical activity, such as walking, yoga, swimming or gentle exercise, helps maintain physical fitness and mental well-being. In addition, a balanced diet and regular medical check-ups are essential to prevent health problems and maintain an optimal energy level.

Balancing Activity and Rest

It is important to find a balance between activity and rest. Retirement does not mean filling every minute of the day with commitments. Taking time to relax, read a book, listen to music or simply enjoy peace and quiet is just as important. A good balance helps to maintain emotional and physical well-being.

Involving the family

Retirement also offers the opportunity to spend more time with the family. Taking an active part in the lives of your children and grandchildren, organizing family gatherings, or simply spending time together can strengthen family ties and create precious memories.

In conclusion, planning leisure time during retirement requires a combination of personal reflection, organization and flexibility. By embracing one's passions, exploring new adventures, maintaining an active social life and taking care of one's health, it is possible to create a meaningful and fulfilling retirement life. The key is to find a balance that allows you to fully enjoy this new phase of life.

Setting New Goals and Priorities

Retirement is a phase of life in which one can review and set new goals and priorities. This shift offers a chance to refocus on what matters most and to invest time and energy in following passions and aspirations that were possibly neglected throughout the working years. Here is how to approach this process effectively.

<u>Personal reflection</u>

The first step in setting new goals and priorities is personal reflection. Taking time to consider what you really want from life is crucial. Asking yourself what activities bring joy and satisfaction, what you want to learn and what experiences you want to have can provide clear direction. It is helpful to write down these thoughts and reflections in a diary or on a worksheet so that they can be reviewed and refined.

<u>Define Specific Goals</u>

Goals should be specific and measurable. For example, instead of saying 'I want to travel more', a specific goal could be 'I want to visit five new cities in the UK within the next year'. This makes the goal concrete and provides a clear path to follow. Specific goals also help to maintain motivation and measure progress.

<u>Prioritize Activities</u>

Prioritizing is crucial once the goals have been established. Not all objectives will have the same weight or urgency. Some might be long-term, such as learning a new language, while others might be short-term, such as taking part in a cookery course. Determining which goals are more important or urgent helps focus energy and avoid feeling overwhelmed.

Create an Action Plan

After setting goals and priorities, it is crucial to create a detailed action plan. This should outline the precise actions required to accomplish each goal, the materials needed, and the estimated time needed. A well-structured plan helps turn abstract goals into concrete actions. For example, if the goal is to stay fit, the plan could include joining a gym, planning weekly exercise sessions and joining a local walking group.

Maintain Flexibility

It is important to maintain flexibility in the pursuit of goals. Circumstances may change and new interests may emerge. Being open to review and adapt goals according to new situations and discoveries allows you to stay aligned with what is truly meaningful. Retirement should be a period of continuous exploration and growth, not rigidly bound to a set plan.

Seek Support and Advice

There is no need to go through this process alone. Seeking support and advice from friends, family or interest groups can be very helpful. Participating in workshops, seminars or discussion groups can offer new perspectives and ideas. In addition, talking to people who have already gone through this transition can provide valuable advice and inspiration.

Celebrating Successes

Achieving goals, big or small, deserves to be celebrated. Recognizing and celebrating successes helps to maintain motivation and provide a sense of achievement. Celebrations need not be elaborate; even small personal celebrations can have a big impact on morale.

Balancing Expectations

Finally, it is important to balance expectations. Retirement is a period of adaptation and discovery. Not all goals will be achieved immediately and not all plans will proceed smoothly. Accepting this and maintaining a positive and resilient mindset is crucial to fully enjoy this phase of life.

In conclusion, setting new goals and priorities during retirement requires reflection, planning and flexibility. With a thoughtful approach, this phase can become a time of great personal growth, satisfaction and happiness.

Chapter 2: Discovering the UK: Travel and Exploration

Retirement is the perfect time to embark on journeys and discoveries that may have been put off for years. Without the obligation to adhere to a rigid work routine, a new phase of life opens up, full of opportunities to explore the beauty and wonders of the UK. This chapter is dedicated to those who wish to rediscover their own country, discovering fascinating and often little-known locations and experiencing adventures that will enrich their lives and culture.

The Wealth of the British Landscape

The UK offers an amazing variety of landscapes, from the rugged Cornish coastline to the rolling hills of the Cotswolds, from the wild Scottish Highlands to picturesque Welsh villages. Every area has an own personality and allure that beg to be discovered. Travelling through these lands allows you to immerse yourself in unspoilt nature and breathe in the history that permeates every corner of the country.

Historic Cities

The UK is famous for its historic cities, each with its own story to tell. London, with its iconic monuments such as Big Ben, Buckingham Palace and the British Museum, is just the beginning. Cities such as Edinburgh, with its majestic castle and the Royal Mile, Bath, famous for its Roman baths and Georgian architecture, and York, with its medieval walls and magnificent Gothic cathedral, are mandatory stops for those wishing to immerse themselves in British history and culture.

Villages and Lesser-Known Locations

In addition to famous cities, the UK is dotted with lesser-known villages and towns that offer unique experiences. Places like Whitby, a charming fishing village in Yorkshire, or Castle Combe, often referred to as the most beautiful village in England, offer a glimpse into rural British life. These places are perfect for those seeking tranquility, scenic beauty and a sense of community that is often lacking in big cities.

Nature Explorations

For nature lovers, the UK is a true paradise. National parks, such as the Lake District, the Peak District and Snowdonia, offer endless opportunities for hiking, walking and outdoor activities. These places are not only beautiful to see, but also offer an opportunity to regenerate and reconnect with nature. Coastlines, such as the Jurassic Coast in Dorset, offer breathtaking views and the chance to discover ancient fossils.

Themed Trips

An interesting way to explore the UK is through thematic trips. Literature enthusiasts can follow in the footsteps of famous authors such as Jane Austen in Bath, William Shakespeare in Stratford-upon-Avon or the Brontë sisters in Yorkshire. History buffs can visit World War II sites such as the Churchill War Rooms in London or Bletchley Park, home of the famous Enigma code. Foodies can embark on a tour of craft breweries or whisky distilleries in Scotland.

Travelling in company

The guesthouse is also an opportunity to travel with friends, family or organized groups. Travelling with others can make the experience even more enjoyable and allow you to share unforgettable moments. There are many travel agencies specializing in tours for retirees that offer tailor-made packages, guaranteeing comfort and safety.

Planning and Useful Resources

Good planning is essential to make the most of travel and exploration. This chapter will provide practical advice on how to organize trips, from accommodation reservations to transport, from must-see attractions to restaurants where you can enjoy local cuisine. It will also suggest useful resources, such as websites, apps and travel guides, to make planning easier and more enjoyable.

In conclusion, the UK offers a myriad of possibilities for travelling and exploring during retirement. With a combination of historic cities, picturesque villages, breathtaking natural landscapes and themed trips, every retiree can find something that resonates with their interests and desires. This chapter is just the beginning of a journey that promises to enrich and inspire, opening up new perspectives and creating lasting memories.

The Hidden Gems of the United Kingdom

The United Kingdom is known for its famous tourist destinations such as London, Edinburgh and the Scottish Highlands. However, in addition to these renowned attractions, the country is home to a multitude of hidden gems that offer unique and often less crowded experiences. Exploring these locations can prove to be an extraordinary journey of discovery, revealing the authentic charm and hidden beauty of the UK. Here are some of the most fascinating hidden gems that every retiree should consider visiting.

Rye, East Sussex

East Sussex's Rye is a picturesque mediaeval village distinguished by its half-timbered homes and cobblestone streets. Mermaid Street, with its picturesque houses and historic inns, seems straight out of a fairy tale. Rye offers a combination of history, culture and nature, with attractions such as Camber Castle, the beautiful gardens of Great Dixter and the nature reserves of Rye Harbour. The town is also famous for its antique shops, cozy cafes and literary festivals.

Pembrokeshire, Wales

The county of Pembrokeshire in south-west Wales is a spectacular but often overlooked destination. The Pembrokeshire coastline, with its 300 kilometers of coastal paths, offers some of the most breathtaking seascapes in the UK. The beaches of Barafundle Bay and Marloes Sands are often considered among the best in the country. Pembrokeshire is also rich in historic castles, such as Pembroke Castle, and picturesque fishing villages such as Tenby, with its colorful houses and sheltered bay.

The Cotswolds

While the Cotswolds is known as a popular tourist destination, many of its gems remain less well known. Villages such as Bibury, described by William

Morris as 'the most beautiful village in England', and Castle Combe, often used as a film set, offer an authentic experience of the English countryside. The Cotswolds are perfect for leisurely walks, exploring ancient churches and historic houses, and sampling local produce at farmers' markets.

Whitby, Yorkshire

Situated on the North Yorkshire coast, Whitby is a charming coastal town with a history associated with Bram Stoker's famous novel 'Dracula'. The town is dominated by the ruins of Whitby Abbey, which offers breathtaking panoramic views. Whitby is also known for its picturesque harbour, delicious fish and chips and its jewelers working with jet, a local semi-precious stone. Each year, the town hosts events such as the Whitby Goth Weekend, attracting visitors with varied interests.

Northumberland

Northumberland, England's northernmost county, is one of the country's least explored but most fascinating regions. With a spectacular coastline and pristine beaches such as Bamburgh Beach, dominated by the majestic Bamburgh Castle, Northumberland offers breathtaking scenery and a rich history. The Northumberland National Park, with its incredibly starry night skies, is a paradise for nature and astronomy lovers. The region is also home to the historic Lindisfarne Island, which can only be reached at low tide.

Shropshire

Shropshire is a quiet and picturesque county on the border with Wales, known for its rolling hills and historic villages. Ludlow, with its medieval castle and farmer's market, is a perfect hidden gem for history and food lovers. Shropshire's hills, such as The Wrekin and Stiperstones, offer wonderful opportunities for hiking and scenic walks. Shropshire is also famous for its industrial heritage, with the Ironbridge Valley Museum, a UNESCO World Heritage Site.

In conclusion, exploring the hidden gems of the UK allows for authentic experiences away from the tourist crowds. These locations offer a unique combination of history, culture, nature and tranquility, making them perfect for retirees wishing to discover new wonders in their own country. With an adventurous approach and an open mind, every corner of the UK can reveal surprises and hidden beauty, creating precious and unforgettable memories.

Train Journeys to Discover the English Countryside

The train is a means of transport that evokes a sense of adventure and romance. Travelling by train through the English countryside allows you to explore breathtaking landscapes, visit picturesque villages and immerse yourself in British history and culture in a comfortable and relaxing way. This way of travelling offers the chance to see the heart of England, with its green hills, flower-filled fields and charming historic towns. Here are some of the most impressive rail routes to discover the English countryside.

The Great Western Railway: London to Penzance

The Great Western Railway (GWR) is one of the oldest and most fascinating railway lines in the UK. Starting from London Paddington, the train travels through the West Country region, passing historic cities such as Bath, famous for its Roman baths and Georgian architecture, and Bristol, with its rich maritime heritage. Continuing westwards, the train heads into the picturesque county of Cornwall, ending in Penzance. During the journey, passengers can enjoy spectacular views of the English countryside, passing through rolling hills and rugged coastlines.

The Settle-Carlisle Railway: A Journey into the Heart of Yorkshire

The Settle-Carlisle Railway is considered one of the most scenic railway lines in the UK. This route runs through the heart of the Yorkshire Dales and Cumbria Fells, offering breathtaking views of some of England's most spectacular scenery. The journey includes a crossing of the Ribblehead Viaduct, a Victorian engineering masterpiece with 24 arches spanning a mountainous landscape. Along the way, passengers can admire rolling hills, sparkling rivers and ancient stone villages.

The Cotswold Line: Oxford to Hereford

The Cotswold Line connects Oxford, one of the world's most famous university cities, with Hereford, passing through the beautiful countryside of the Cotswolds. This route allows you to explore a region renowned for its picturesque stone villages, historic gardens and traditional markets. Stops such as Moreton-in-Marsh and Evesham offer the opportunity to disembark and visit charming places, take walks in the hills and savor the tranquility of rural life.

Shrewsbury to Swansea on the Heart of Wales Line

A train track that passes through some of Wales' most isolated and intriguing regions is called the Heart of Wales Line. Starting in Shrewsbury, the train winds its way through the Welsh countryside, passing green hills, deep valleys and picturesque villages. Stops along the way, such as Llandrindod Wells and Llanwrtyd Wells, offer a taste of Welsh culture and history. Swansea, a seaside city with a thriving cultural life and stunning beaches, is where the adventure comes to an end.

The East Coast Main Line connects Edinburgh with London

For those who want a longer journey, the East Coast Main Line offers an extraordinary experience, connecting London to Edinburgh. This route traverses the countryside of the East and North of England, offering views of great beauty and stops in historic cities such as York, with its impressive Gothic cathedral, and Durham, famous for its castle and cathedral. The journey continues north, crossing the spectacular Northumberland coast and ending in Scotland's historic capital, Edinburgh.

Practical Tips for Train Travel

To make the most of rail travel through the English countryside, it is useful to plan ahead. Buying tickets online can often be cheaper and guarantee reserved seats. Taking a travel guide or app with you to learn more about stops and attractions along the way can enrich the experience. In addition, travelling off-peak can offer a quieter and more relaxing experience.

In conclusion, rail travel through the English countryside offers a unique and fascinating way to explore the UK. With spectacular landscapes, historic towns and picturesque villages, each route promises unforgettable adventures and a deep connection with the country's natural and cultural beauty.

Coastal Routes: Beaches and Cliffs

The UK, with its spectacular and varied coastline, offers a plethora of coastal itineraries that allow you to discover enchanting beaches, breathtaking cliffs and picturesque fishing villages. These routes are ideal for those seeking outdoor adventures, picture-postcard landscapes and moments of pure tranquility. Here is a detailed overview of some of the UK's most fascinating coastal routes.

The Jurassic Coast, Dorset and Devon

A UNESCO World Heritage Site, the Jurassic Coast extends 95 miles down England's south coast from Devon's Exmouth to Dorset's Studland Bay. This section of the coast is well-known for its unusual geological formations and prehistoric fossils. The limestone cliffs of Old Harry Rocks and the beautiful beach at Durdle Door, with its iconic natural arch, are among the main attractions. Along the way, towns such as Lyme Regis and Charmouth offer opportunities to search for fossils and discover fascinating geological museums.

The Northumberland Coast

The Northumberland Coast in north-east England is one of the UK's least crowded but most fascinating coastal areas. This itinerary includes unspoilt beaches, historic castles and nature reserves. Bamburgh Beach, with its imposing medieval castle silhouetted against the golden sand, offers breathtaking views. Holy Island, or Lindisfarne, only accessible at low tide, is famous for its monastery and rich history. The Farne Islands nature reserve is a paradise for wildlife lovers, with colonies of seals and a variety of seabirds.

The Gower Peninsula, Wales

The first place in the UK to be named an Area of Outstanding Natural Beauty (AONB) was the Gower Peninsula in south Wales. It offers spectacular beaches, rugged cliffs and breathtaking scenery. Many people rank Rhossili Bay as one of the world's top beaches because of its expansive sand dunes and waves that are ideal for surfing. Another feature is Three Cliffs Bay, which has distinctive sand dunes and rock formations. The peninsula also offers numerous hiking trails that allow you to explore the coast on foot.

The Causeway Coast, Northern Ireland

The Causeway Coast in County Antrim is famous for its dramatic landscape and historic attractions. The hexagon-shaped basalt columns of the Giant's Causeway, a UNESCO World Heritage Site, were created by past volcanic eruptions. The coastal path leading to the Carrick-a-Rede rope bridge offers spectacular views of the ocean and cliffs. The ruins of Dunluce Castle, perched on a rocky headland, add a touch of mystery and history to the route.

The Wild Atlantic Way, Scotland

The Wild Atlantic Way is one of the UK's most spectacular and wild coastal routes, stretching along the west coast of Scotland. This route offers breathtaking views of vertiginous cliffs, deserted beaches and remote islands. The cliffs of Cape Wrath, Scotland's most north-westerly point, offer incredible views of the Atlantic Ocean. The Outer Hebrides, with islands such as Lewis and Harris, are famous for their white beaches and rugged landscapes. Along the way, visitors can discover ancient ruins, lonely lighthouses and traditional fishing villages.

Practical Tips for Exploring the Coast

Exploring the UK coast requires good planning. It is advisable to check the weather forecast and dress appropriately for changing weather conditions. Carrying detailed maps and using navigation apps can be helpful in finding your way along coastal paths. In addition, many of these areas offer accommodation such as B&Bs, cottages and campsites, allowing you to stay comfortably close to the main attractions.

In conclusion, trips along the UK's coastal routes offer an unforgettable experience, allowing you to discover enchanting beaches and spectacular cliffs. Each route has its own unique character and wonders to explore, providing exciting adventures and moments of pure natural beauty. Whether a leisurely stroll along a deserted beach or an adventurous hike over vertiginous cliffs, the British coast has something to offer every traveler.

Historical Trips: Castles, Abbeys and Monuments

The UK is a treasure trove of history and culture, with a myriad of majestic castles, serene abbeys and monuments that tell the rich and complex history of the British Isles. Exploring these historic sites offers a journey through time, allowing you to relive past eras and better understand the present. Here is a detailed overview of some of the most significant historical places to visit.

Castles

Windsor Castle, Berkshire

William the Conqueror established Windsor fortress in the eleventh century, making it the oldest and biggest inhabited fortress on Earth. The castle, which is one of the Queen's official homes, provides an interesting look into British royal history. Visitors can explore the sumptuous State Apartments, St George's Chapel, which houses the tombs of numerous monarchs, and the beautiful castle grounds.

Edinburgh Castle, Scotland

One of Scotland's most popular historic sites, Edinburgh Castle is perched atop an old volcanic rock that dominates the city skyline. Its history dates back to the 7th century and it has played a crucial role in Scottish history. Highlights include the Stone of Destiny, used for the coronations of Scottish kings, the War Prisons and the Scottish Crown Jewels.

Cardiff Castle, Wales

Cardiff Castle is a fascinating mix of Roman, Norman and Victorian Gothic history. Located in the heart of the Welsh capital, the castle offers a unique experience with its historic walls, Norman ramparts and opulent

Victorian rooms. Visitors can also explore the air raid shelters used during World War II.

Abbeys

Westminster Abbey, London

Westminster Abbey is one of the most important and historically significant places of worship in the UK. Founded in A.D. 960, the abbey has been the coronation place of British monarchs since 1066 and houses the tombs of numerous illustrious monarchs, poets and scientists, including Isaac Newton and Charles Darwin. Its Gothic architecture and stained-glass windows offer an extraordinary visual experience.

Glastonbury Abbey, Somerset

Glastonbury Abbey is shrouded in mystery and legend, with stories linking it to King Arthur and the Holy Grail. Founded in the 7th century, it is one of the oldest and most storied abbeys in England. Although now in ruins, the abbey retains a special charm with its picturesque ruins and tranquil gardens.

Melrose Abbey, Scotland

Located in the Scottish Borders, Melrose Abbey is an outstanding example of Gothic architecture. Founded in 1136 by Cistercian monks, the abbey is famous for being the burial place of the embalmed heart of Robert I of Scotland, also known as Robert the Bruce. Its detailed ruins offer a fascinating insight into medieval monastic life.

Monuments

Stonehenge, Wiltshire

Dating back to around 3000 BC, Stonehenge is one of the most famous prehistoric monuments in the world. This mysterious stone circle has fascinated and baffled archaeologists for centuries. Located in the Salisbury Plain, Stonehenge is surrounded by a landscape rich in other Neolithic and Bronze Age structures. Visitors can explore the site and the nearby visitor center, which offers insights into the history and significance of the monument.

Hadrian's Wall, Northern England

Hadrian's Wall is an imposing Roman fortification built under Emperor Hadrian in the 2nd century AD. The wall stretches 73 miles from coast to coast in northern England and was built to defend the Roman province of Britain from northern tribes. The remains of forts, watchtowers and settlements along the wall provide an extraordinary insight into life on the border of the Roman Empire.

Bannockburn Monument, Scotland

The Bannockburn Monument commemorates the battle of 1314, in which the Scottish army under Robert the Bruce defeated the English army during the First War of Scottish Independence. Located near Stirling, the site houses an interactive visitor center that allows visitors to relive the battle and understand the historical significance of the event.

Exploring castles, abbeys and monuments in the UK offers an immersive journey into the country's rich history. Each site tells a unique story, from royal and religious power to conquests and wars. Visiting these places allows you to better understand the UK's historical roots and appreciate the beauty and complexity of its cultural heritage.

Exploring lesser-known locations

Dartmoor National Park

Dartmoor National Park, located in Devon, England, is a vast area of wild moors, bogs, granite hills and ancient villages. This fascinating region offers a variety of outdoor activities, breathtaking scenery and a rich cultural history. Here is a detailed guide on how to get to Dartmoor, where to stay, what to eat and what to see.

How to get there

- By Car: Dartmoor is easily accessible by car, with several main roads running through it. From London, the most direct route is via the M4 and M5 to Exeter, and then following signs to the park.

From Exeter, there are several roads leading to different parts of Dartmoor, including the A38 and A30.
- By Train: The main railway stations near Dartmoor are Exeter, Newton Abbot and Plymouth. To explore the park, you can rent a car or take a bus from these stations. Train travel takes around 2.5 hours from London Paddington to Exeter.
- By Bus: There are regular bus services connecting Exeter, Plymouth and other Devon towns to Dartmoor. Local buses can take you to villages and attractions within the park.

Where to stay

- Hotels and B&Bs: Dartmoor offers a variety of accommodation, from luxurious country hotels to quaint bed and breakfasts. Some of the best hotels include Bovey Castle, a luxurious resort located in the heart of the park, and Gidleigh Park, known for its Michelin-starred restaurant.
- Cottages and Holiday Homes: For a more independent experience, there are numerous cottages and holiday homes available for rent. These can provide a comfortable and cozy base for exploring the park.
- Campsites: Dartmoor is a paradise for campers, with numerous well-equipped campsites scattered throughout the park. Some of the most popular campsites include River Dart Country Park and Langstone Manor Holiday Park.

What to Eat

- Restaurants: Dartmoor boasts a number of excellent restaurants offering dishes prepared with local ingredients. In addition to the aforementioned Gidleigh Park, it is worth visiting The Cornish Arms in Tavistock, a traditional pub with excellent food.
- Cafes and Afternoon Teas: For an authentic experience, try an afternoon tea in one of the many cafes and tea rooms in the park. The Two Bridges Hotel and Warren House Inn offer charming tea breaks with panoramic views.

- Local produce: Don't miss the local markets and farms where you can buy fresh, artisanal produce. Local cheeses, Dartmoor lamb and artisan baked goods are a must try.

What to see

- Moorlands and Fens: Dartmoor is famous for its open moors and fens. Hikes in the granite hills, known as 'tors', offer spectacular views. Haytor and Hound Tor are among the most famous and accessible tors.
- Historical Sites: The park is rich in history with ancient monuments and villages. Merrivale is an archaeological site with ancient stones and circles. The village of Widecombe-in-the-Moor is known for its picturesque church and annual fair.
- Outdoor Activities: Dartmoor is ideal for hiking, cycling, climbing and birdwatching. The Dart and Teign rivers offer opportunities for fishing and boating.
- Wildlife: The park is home to a variety of wildlife, including Dartmoor ponies, deer, and a wide range of birds. A guided hike can offer a greater understanding of the local ecosystem.
- Museums and Visitor Centres: The Dartmoor National Park Visitor Centre in Princetown offers informative exhibitions on the history and geology of the park. The Museum of Dartmoor Life in Okehampton provides further insights into local life and agricultural history.

In conclusion, Dartmoor National Park offers a unique combination of natural beauty, historical riches and a wide range of outdoor activities. Dartmoor offers something for everyone, whether you're searching for exhilarating experiences or a peaceful getaway in the great outdoors.

The Scilly Isles

The Isles of Scilly are an archipelago of exceptional natural beauty and historical significance, situated off the southwest coast of England. With their pristine beaches, crystal clear waters and tranquil atmosphere, the

Scillys are a perfect destination for those seeking a relaxing getaway or an outdoor adventure. Here is a detailed guide on how to get to the islands, where to stay, what to eat and what to see.

How to get there

- By Air: The quickest way to reach the Isles of Scilly is via a flight from Exeter, Newquay or Land's End. The main airline serving the islands is Skybus, which offers regular flights to St Mary's airport, the main island of Scilly. Flights take between 15 and 60 minutes, depending on the city of departure.
- By Ship: For those who prefer to travel by sea, the Scillonian III ferry departs from Penzance and arrives in St. Mary's. The journey takes about 2 hours and 45 minutes, offering spectacular views of the Cornish coastline and the islands themselves. It is best to get tickets in advance during the busiest times of year.

Where to Stay

- Hotels: There are many different lodging options available on the Isles of Scilly, ranging from opulent boutique hotels to quaint guesthouses. The Tresco Abbey Garden Hotel, located on Tresco Island, is known for its beautiful gardens and breathtaking views. The Star Castle Hotel, located on St. Mary's, offers a unique historical experience, being a 16th century castle converted into a luxury hotel.
- Cottages and Apartments: For those seeking a more independent stay, there are numerous cottages and flats available for rent. These accommodations offer a convenient base for exploring the islands at your own pace. The islands of St. Martin's and St. Agnes have several fascinating options for visitors.
- Campsites: For the more adventurous, there are campsites available on some of the islands. The Garrison Campsite on St. Mary's offers panoramic views and a peaceful atmosphere. Campers can enjoy all the necessary amenities while being surrounded by nature.

What to Eat

- Restaurants and Cafes: The Isles of Scilly are renowned for their fresh produce and local cuisine. Tresco's Ruin Beach Café is well-known for its mouthwatering seafood specialities and breathtaking views of the ocean. The Mermaid Inn on St. Mary's is a traditional pub offering a wide range of classic British dishes.
- Local Markets: For those who prefer to cook for themselves, local markets offer a selection of fresh fish, farm produce and other local ingredients. The Farmer's Market on St Mary's is a great place to find fresh, artisan produce.
- Local Dishes: Dishes not to be missed include seafood specialities such as lobster and crab from the Scillys, and Cornish meat pies.

What to See

- Tresco Abbey Gardens: One of the highlights of the Isles of Scilly is the Tresco Abbey Garden, a sub-tropical garden housing a wide range of exotic plants from around the world. The gardens are an oasis of color and fragrance, ideal for a relaxing stroll.
- Unspoilt Beaches: The Isles of Scilly boast some of the most beautiful beaches in the UK. Among the best are Great Bay on St. Martin's, Porthcressa Beach on St. Mary's and Appletree Bay on Tresco. White sand and turquoise waters make these beaches ideal for lounging, swimming, and snorkelling.
- Hiking Trails: The islands are a hiker's paradise, with numerous trails passing through breathtaking scenery. St. Mary's Coastal Path offers spectacular views of the ocean and wilderness. Each island has its own unique trails, suitable for all abilities.
- Historical Sites: The Isles of Scilly are rich in history, with numerous archaeological and historical sites to explore. Of these, the prehistoric site of Bant's Carn on St Mary's and the ruins of Cromwell's Castle on Tresco are particularly fascinating.
- Water Activities: For water sports enthusiasts, the Isles of Scilly offer numerous opportunities for kayaking, sailing and

paddleboarding. The calm, crystal-clear waters are ideal for exploring the coastline and hidden bays.

In conclusion, the Isles of Scilly offer a unique and unforgettable experience, combining natural beauty, fascinating history and culinary delights. Whether you are looking for adventure, relaxation or cultural exploration, this archipelago has something to offer everyone.

Villages of the Cotswolds

The Cotswolds, a hilly region in the heart of England, is famous for its charming honey-coloured stone villages, undulating landscapes and rich and fascinating history. This detailed guide will help you discover how to get to the region, where to stay, what to eat and what to see in the picturesque villages of the Cotswolds.

How to get there

- By Car: The Cotswolds region is easily accessible by car. It is about two hours from London, following the M40 to Oxford and then taking local roads to the villages. Even from Birmingham and Bristol, the journey is short and convenient, making the Cotswolds a perfect destination for a weekend trip.
- By Train: Several towns in the Cotswolds are well connected to London by rail service. The Great Western Railway offers frequent trains from Paddington to Moreton-in-Marsh, one of the main access points to the region, with a journey time of around 90 minutes. From there, you can take local buses or taxis to explore the surrounding villages.
- By Bus: National Express and Stagecoach buses connect several towns in the UK with the Cotswolds. Once in Cheltenham or Gloucester, it is easy to get around with local bus services.
- Where to Stay
- Hotels and Inns: The Cotswolds offer a wide range of accommodation, from luxurious country hotels to cozy historic inns. The Lygon Arms on Broadway, a hotel with a history of over

600 years, offers a luxury experience with a historic touch. The Slaughters Manor House, located in the picturesque village of Lower Slaughter, is another upmarket option with a gourmet restaurant.
- B&B and Holiday Homes: For a more intimate and authentic experience, bed and breakfasts and holiday homes are ideal. You can find charming cottages in villages such as Bourton-on-the-Water and Chipping Campden, which offer modern comforts in traditional settings.
- Campsites: For those who like to be in touch with nature, there are several well-equipped campsites in the region, such as Cotswold Farm Park, which offers a combination of farmhouse and camping.

What to Eat

- Local Cuisine: The cuisine of the Cotswolds is renowned for its use of fresh, local ingredients. In local pubs and restaurants, you can enjoy traditional dishes such as Cotswold Lamb, locally reared lamb, and artisan cheeses such as Double Gloucester.
- Restaurants: Some of the best restaurants include The Wild Rabbit in Kingham, a contemporary pub with a Michelin star, and The Feathered Nest Country Inn in Nether Westcote, which offers fine dining in a rustic setting.
- Afternoon Tea: You can't visit the Cotswolds without trying a traditional afternoon tea. The Old Bakery Tea Room in Stow-on-the-Wold is famous for its fresh scones and wide selection of teas.

What To See

- Picturesque Villages: The villages of the Cotswolds are the real heart of the region. Bourton-on-the-With its canals, Water—dubbed the "Venice of the Cotswolds"—is the ideal place for a leisurely stroll. With its historic stone homes, Bibury—dubbed "the most beautiful village in England" by William Morris—offers a charming landscape.

- Historic Sites: The Cotswolds are rich in history. Visit Sudeley Castle in Winchcombe, a historic mansion with magnificent gardens and a long royal history. St Edward's Church in Stow-on-the-Wold, with its fairy-tale doorway lined with ancient trees, is another must-see.
- Gardens and Parks: Hidcote Manor Garden, one of the UK's most celebrated gardens, offers a unique experience with its themed spaces and green architecture. The Batsford Arboretum near Moreton-in-Marsh is perfect for a relaxing walk among the exotic trees and seasonal flowers.
- Outdoor Activities: The Cotswolds region is ideal for lovers of outdoor activities. Hiking along the Cotswold Way, a trail that winds through breathtaking scenery, and cycling through the hills and picturesque villages are among the most rewarding experiences.

To sum up, the Cotswold villages provide the ideal fusion of stunning scenery, an intriguing past, and distinctive regional culture. The Cotswolds provide something for everyone, whether your goals are leisure, adventure, or cultural discovery.

Themed trips, such as literary trails inspired by famous British authors

The UK, with its rich literary history, offers plenty of opportunities for travelers wishing to immerse themselves in the places that inspired some of Britain's greatest authors. Literary trails are a fascinating way to explore the cultural and geographical landscape that gave birth to unforgettable works. Here are some of the best-known literary routes in Britain.

1. The Jane Austen Trail

Jane Austen is one of the best-loved writers in English literature, and her work is intrinsically linked to the places where she lived. The Jane Austen Centre in Bath is a great starting point for exploring the spa town where Austen spent part of her life and set some of her novels, including 'Persuasion' and 'Northanger Abbey'. After a visit to the museum, stroll along Bath's Georgian streets, including the Royal Crescent and The Circus, to get a taste of life in Austen's time. You can also visit Austen's home in Chawton, Hampshire, where she wrote many of her masterpieces.

2. William Wordsworth's Lake District

The Lake District is famous for its natural beauty and for being the muse of romantic poet William Wordsworth. Dove Cottage in Grasmere, where Wordsworth lived from 1799 to 1808, is now a museum dedicated to his life and work. Visitors can explore the gardens and house, as well as follow paths leading to Lake Grasmere and Lake Rydal, places that inspired many of his poems. Another must-see is Rydal Mount, Wordsworth's residence for much of his adult life.

3. The Brontë Lands

The Brontë sisters, Emily, Charlotte and Anne, are deeply associated with the wild Yorkshire moors. The Brontë Parsonage Museum in Haworth is the residence where the sisters resided and penned their well-known books, including "Jane Eyre" and "Wuthering Heights." The village of Haworth and the surrounding footpaths offer an exciting journey into the heart of the moors that so influenced their writing. Visitors can walk the paths leading to Top Withens, the isolated house said to have inspired 'Wuthering Heights'.

4. Sir Walter Scott's Edinburgh

Sir Walter Scott, one of Scotland's greatest historical novelists, left an indelible mark on Edinburgh. The Scott Monument, located in Princes Street Gardens, is an impressive tribute to the poet and novelist. For a more intimate experience, visit Abbotsford House, Scott's residence, located near Melrose. The house is a museum dedicated to his life and works, with an impressive collection of manuscripts, rare books and personal items.

5. J.R.R. Tolkien's Oxfordshire

For fantasy fans, a visit to the places associated with J.R.R. Tolkien is a must. Although Tolkien was born in South Africa, he spent most of his life in Oxford, where he taught at university. Fans can visit The Eagle and

Child pub, also known as The Bird and Baby, where Tolkien and his colleagues from the Inklings literary group met regularly. Another important stop is Tolkien's home on Northmoor Road, where he wrote 'The Hobbit' and much of 'The Lord of the Rings'.

Literary trails in the UK offer a unique opportunity to get in touch with the places that inspired some of the greatest masterpieces of English literature. Each route offers not only a deep immersion into the lives and work of the authors, but also a discovery of the natural and historical beauty of the UK. Whether you are a fan of Victorian novels, romantic poetry or epic fantasy worlds, there is a literary trail waiting to be explored.

Chapter 3 Recreational Activities and Hobbies

Retirement represents a phase of life characterized by greater freedom and availability of time, offering a unique opportunity to explore new passions and rediscover long neglected interests. After years devoted to work and family responsibilities, many retirees find leisure time a valuable ally in improving their quality of life, keeping active and socially involved. This chapter is devoted to exploring a wide range of recreational activities and hobbies that can enrich the lives of pensioners in the UK.

The Value of Recreational Activities

Numerous studies have shown that maintaining an active mind and body is essential for a healthy and fulfilling life in retirement. Recreational activities not only provide fun and relaxation but can also help improve mental and physical health. Taking part in hobbies and pastimes can reduce stress, prevent depression and foster a sense of personal fulfilment. In addition, many recreational activities promote social interaction, helping retirees build new friendships and maintain a vital support network.

Exploring New Horizons

Retirement offers the perfect opportunity to explore new horizons. Whether it's learning to play a musical instrument, taking up painting or cultivating a vegetable garden, the possibilities are endless. Creative hobbies such as drawing, writing or do-it-yourself can be particularly rewarding, allowing you to express yourself and develop new skills. For those who love nature, activities such as gardening, bird watching or walks in the English countryside offer a wonderful way to connect with the environment and enjoy the beauty of the British landscape.

Physical and Sporting Activities

Maintaining regular physical activity is essential for well-being in retirement. The Cotswolds, with their picturesque villages and trails, offer the ideal backdrop for hiking, cycling and walking. In addition, many pensioners find pleasure in light sports such as golf, swimming or tennis, which allow them to keep fit without excessive effort. Municipal swimming pools, sports centers and golf clubs often have facilities and programmes specifically designed for the elderly, making participation easy and enjoyable.

Social and Community Activities

Social and community activities play a crucial role in keeping the network of interpersonal relationships alive. Book clubs, voluntary groups and local associations offer countless opportunities to meet new people and actively contribute to the community. Participating in social and cultural events, such as theatre performances, concerts and art exhibitions, can enrich daily life and provide new cultural stimuli. In addition, many municipalities in the UK organize courses and workshops on a wide range of topics, from foreign languages to local history, offering the opportunity to continue learning and growing.

Choosing the Right Hobbies

Choosing the right hobbies and leisure activities is a personal decision that depends on one's inclinations, abilities and physical condition. It is important to consider what brings you joy and satisfaction, and not be afraid to experiment with different activities until you find the ones that resonate the most. For some, this might mean taking up a hobby they have always wanted to try but never had the time to do; for others, it might mean rediscovering a passion from their youth.

In conclusion, leisure activities and hobbies can turn retirement into a time of personal growth, exploration and happiness. This chapter will offer a detailed overview of the various options available, providing practical tips and inspiration to help retirees make the most of their free time. From arts and crafts activities to light sports and outdoor adventures, there are endless possibilities for living a full and fulfilling retirement in the UK.

Gardening: From Garden Design to Practical Advice

Gardening is more than just a pastime; it is an art that combines creativity, science and care. Creating a garden requires planning, attention to detail and a little patience. In this guide, we explore how to turn your outdoor space into a green oasis, from the first steps of the project to practical tips for daily maintenance.

Designing the Garden

1. Assessing the Space

The first step in designing a garden is to evaluate the available space. Consider the size of your garden, sun exposure, soil quality and the local climate. Draw a plan of the garden, indicating sunny and shady areas, drainage points and any existing features such as trees, walls or fences.

2. Choice of Theme

The theme of the garden will influence the type of plants and furnishings. A flower garden, veggie garden, rock garden, or water garden are your options. Each theme has its own particularities and requires specific plants and particular designs. For example, a flower garden requires a variety of perennials and annuals, while a vegetable garden will need raised beds and a composting area.

3. Plant selection

The selection of plants is essential. Choose plants that will grow well in your climate and require minimal upkeep in line with your lifestyle. Mixing perennials, annuals, shrubs and trees can create an interesting and varied garden all year round. Also consider native plants, which tend to be hardier and require less care.

4. Layout planning

Once the plants have been selected, plan the layout of the garden. Arrange the plants so that taller plants do not overshadow lower ones. Create paths to facilitate access and movement within the garden. Consider adding ornamental features like benches, statues, and fountains.

Practical Gardening Tips

1. Soil Preparation

Good soil is the basis of a healthy garden. Work the soil to improve its structure and add compost or manure to enrich it with nutrients. Check the pH of the soil and, if necessary, amend it with lime or sulphur to make it more suitable for your plants.

2. Irrigation

Irrigation is crucial to the success of the garden. Install an automatic irrigation system or use permeable hoses to ensure that the plants receive the right amount of water. Recall that various plants have varying water requirements; for example, succulent plants need less water than flowering plants.

3. Mulching

Mulching helps to maintain soil moisture, prevent weed growth and improve soil structure over time. Use organic materials such as shredded bark, dry leaves or straw. To prevent rot, cover the plants with a 5-7 cm layer of mulch, making sure to leave space around the stems.

4. Pruning and Maintenance

Pruning on a regular basis keeps the plants robust and healthy. To increase air circulation, cut off any diseased or dead branches and trim off any branches that are too crowded. Each type of plant has specific pruning needs, so find out the appropriate techniques for each.

5. Pest control

Monitor the garden regularly for signs of pests or diseases. Use biological control methods, such as the introduction of beneficial insects, or organic products, to reduce environmental impact. Avoid the indiscriminate use of chemical pesticides, which can also harm beneficial insects.

6. Composting

Enhancing garden soil and recycling organic waste can be achieved by composting. Gather leaves, grass clippings, food scraps, and other organic wastes and place them in a compost container. Turn the compost regularly and keep it moist to accelerate the decomposition process.

Gardening is an activity that can bring great satisfaction and numerous benefits, both physical and mental. Whether you are a beginner or an expert, a well-designed and maintained garden can become a place of beauty and tranquility. Planning carefully, choosing the right plants and following the practical tips described can help create a green space that thrives and brings joy for many years to come.

Cooking and Pastry: Traditional and Innovative Recipes

Cooking and baking are culinary arts that offer an infinite variety of taste experiences, blending flavors, traditions and innovations. The United Kingdom, with its rich gastronomic history, offers a wide range of dishes from traditional recipes to more modern and innovative creations. In this text, we explore some of Britain's classic recipes and how they can be reinvented with a contemporary twist.

Traditional Recipes

1. Fish and Chips

Possibly the most famous dish from Britain is fish and chips. Traditionally, this dish consists of fillets of white fish, such as cod or haddock, dipped in a light batter and fried until crispy, accompanied by thick chips. It is frequently served with sea salt, a dash of malt vinegar, and side dishes like mushy peas.

2. Shepherd's Pie

Shepherd's Pie is another classic British comfort food. This savory pie has a filling of minced lamb (or beef, in the Cottage Pie variant) cooked with onions, carrots and peas, covered with a layer of baked golden mashed potatoes. The combination of rich flavors and the creamy texture of the mash makes this dish a favorite in many homes.

3. Scones with Clotted Cream and Marmalade

A must for the traditional afternoon tea, scones are fluffy treats that are served warm, split in half and generously filled with clotted cream and strawberry jam. Scones are simple to prepare and are a perfect treat for a relaxing afternoon.

Innovations in the Kitchen

1. Fish and Chips Revisited

For a modern version of the classic Fish and Chips, you can opt to use a variety of different fish, such as salmon or tuna, and accompany them with baked sweet potato fries. For the batter, try adding spices such as curry or paprika for extra flavor. Accompany with homemade sauces such as a garlic mayonnaise or a spicy tartar sauce.

2. Shepherd's Pie with a Touch of Innovation

An interesting variation of the traditional Shepherd's Pie is to use different ingredients for the filling and topping. For example, replace lamb with turkey or a vegetarian mixture of lentils and mushrooms. For the topping, try mashed cauliflower instead of potatoes for a lighter, low-carbohydrate option.

3. Savoury Scones

For an innovative twist on scones, why not try a savory version? Cheese and herb scones are a great alternative. Add grated cheddar cheese, herbs such as rosemary or thyme and a sprinkle of black pepper to the basic scone mixture. These savory scones are perfect with soups or salads.

Practical Tips for Cooking and Baking

1. Quality Ingredients

Whether a recipe is classic or modern, the key to its success is using fresh, high-quality ingredients. Buy fresh fish from sustainable sources, quality meat and local farm produce to ensure the best possible flavor in your dishes.

2. Adequate equipment

Make sure you have the right equipment for cooking and baking. Tools such as a good set of knives, an accurate kitchen scale, non-stick pans and a planetary mixer can make all the difference in the preparation and presentation of dishes.

3. Experimentation and Creativity

Don't be afraid to experiment and be creative in the kitchen. Try new flavor combinations, cooking techniques and presentations. Cooking is an ever-evolving field, and often the most delicious innovations come from a bit of curiosity and resourcefulness.

4. Sharing and Learning

Cooking and baking are social activities. Involve friends and family in the preparation of dishes, organize themed dinners or exchange recipes with other cooking enthusiasts. Participating in cooking classes or following culinary blogs can provide new ideas and inspiration.

Whether you are fond of traditional recipes or eager to experiment with new ideas, cooking and baking offer plenty of possibilities to explore and enjoy. From classic fish and chips to innovative savory scones, every dish is an opportunity to create something special and share moments of joy with those around you. Enjoy!

Handicrafts: Knitting, Sewing and Crafts

Working with your hands is an activity that offers many benefits, including relaxation, personal satisfaction and the chance to create unique objects. Knitting, sewing and handicrafts are three of the most popular disciplines among handicraft enthusiasts. We explore each of these activities in detail, offering practical tips and inspiration for those who wish to immerse themselves in these creative hobbies.

Knitting

Knitting is an ancient art involving the use of two needles to create fabric by weaving threads of wool or other materials. It is a soothing pastime that you can enjoy anywhere, even on a train ride or in the privacy of your own home.

Tools and Materials: You will need some yarn and a pair of knitting needles to get started. There are different sizes of needles and types of yarn, which vary depending on the project you choose. Beginners may find it useful to start with medium sized needles and medium weight wool yarn, which is easier to handle.

Beginner Projects: Neck warmers, scarves and simple beanies are good projects for beginners. These items allow you to practise basic stitches such as straight stitch and reverse stitch without requiring too much complexity.

Benefits: Besides producing useful and beautiful garments, knitting can improve concentration and reduce stress. The repetitiveness of the movements is calming and can help improve hand-eye coordination.

Sewing

Sewing is a versatile skill that ranges from garment repair to the art of patchwork and the creation of custom-made garments. With a basic set of tools and a little practice, a wide range of projects can be achieved.

Tools and Materials: To get started, you will need a sewing machine, needles, thread, scissors, pins and fabric. Again, it is useful to start with simple projects that do not require too expensive materials.

Beginner Projects: Cushions, simple bags and home accessories are good places to start. These projects help familiarize you with the sewing machine and various sewing techniques such as hemming and straight stitching.

Benefits: Sewing not only allows you to personalize your wardrobe and furniture, but also helps you develop precision and patience. It is an activity that can become a true creative outlet, offering a sense of achievement every time you complete a project.

Crafts

Handicrafts encompass a wide range of activities, from jewellery making to decoupage to woodworking. It is an open field for innovation and personal creativity.

Tools and Materials: Tools vary enormously depending on the type of craft. However, some basic tools include glue, scissors, pliers, paper, paint and materials specific to the chosen project, such as beads for jewellery or wood for woodwork.

Beginner Projects: Simple craft projects include creating handmade cards, beaded bracelets and home decorations. These projects do not require expensive materials and can be completed in a few hours.

Benefits: Crafts stimulate creativity and offer a tangible way to express oneself. It can also be a social activity, where ideas and techniques are shared with friends or by participating in workshops. In addition, crafts can become a source of income by selling one's creations online or at local markets.

Knitting, sewing and crafts are activities that offer an endless range of creative possibilities. Whether creating a warm jumper, repairing a garment or making a decorative object, handicrafts allow you to develop practical skills and enjoy the pleasure of creation. These activities not only enrich leisure time, but also promote mental and physical well-being, making retirement a time full of new discoveries and satisfaction.

Photography and Painting: Expressing Creativity

Photography and painting are two art forms that offer extraordinary ways to express creativity and capture the beauty of the world. Both disciplines allow individuals to explore their artistic potential, develop new skills and see the world from a different perspective. In this text, we will explore how to approach these arts, basic techniques, benefits and ways to get started.

Photography: Capturing Moments

Photography is an art of capturing moments, emotions and scenes through the use of a camera. Whether it is a simple smartphone or a professional camera, photography is accessible to everyone and can be practiced in many different ways.

Basic Tools and Techniques: Understanding how a camera functions is vital to begin shooting photos. It is essential to comprehend ideas like exposure, aperture, shutter speed, and ISO sensitivity. Besides technique, the photographer's eye plays a crucial role; knowing how to observe and compose a scene is what distinguishes a good photo from an extraordinary one.

Themes and Styles: There are many genres of photography, including landscape, portrait, macro, street photography and abstract photography. Each genre requires a different approach and can be explored to find what inspires most. For example, landscape photography often requires patience and the ability to work with natural light, while street photography captures spontaneous moments of everyday life.

Benefits: Using photographs to tell tales and exhibit your creativity is a fantastic use of photography. In addition, it can be a relaxing and meditative activity that helps develop a keen eye for detail and a greater awareness of the world around you.

Painting: Creating with Color and Form

Painting is a kind of art in which colour, shape, and texture are used to convey thoughts and feelings. With a canvas and colors, one can create works ranging from abstract to realism, exploring an infinite range of styles and techniques.

Basic Tools and Techniques: To start painting, you need some essential tools: canvas, brushes, colors (acrylics, oils, watercolours) and a palette for mixing colors. Basic techniques include color washing, using layers to create depth and mixing colors to achieve different tones. Understanding color theory and composition techniques can help improve the quality of works.

Styles and Themes: Painting offers a wide range of styles, such as realism, impressionism, surrealism and abstractionism. Every style has distinct qualities of its own that can be explored based on individual preferences. Subject matter can include still lifes, abstract pieces, and portraits as well as landscapes.

Benefits: Painting is an activity that promotes creativity and freedom of expression. It can be therapeutic, helping to reduce stress and improve mental health. It also offers a way to explore emotions and thoughts in a visual way, creating a connection between the artist and the viewer.

How to Start

Courses and Workshops: Taking photography or painting courses can be a great way to learn basic techniques and get feedback on how to improve. Many communities offer workshops, and numerous free or paid tutorials can be found online.

Practice and Experimentation: Practice is essential to improve in both disciplines. Experimenting with different techniques, styles and instruments helps you find your artistic voice. Do not fear making errors; frequently, the most creative works are the result of trial and error and failure.

Sharing and Feedback: Giving your work to loved ones, friends, or online groups can yield insightful criticism and creative inspiration. You can meet other fans and get support by connecting on social media sites and in artist forums.

Photography and painting are arts that offer countless possibilities to express creativity and discover new perspectives. Whether capturing a breathtaking sunset with a camera or painting a vibrant landscape, both activities allow you to explore your inner world and share it with others. Take advantage of these art forms to enrich your life, find new hobbies and enjoy fulfilling experiences.

Chapter 4 Sport and Well-being

Retirement is a significant transition period in a person's life, an opportunity to explore new interests and engage in activities that bring joy and well-being. Sport and wellness play a crucial role in this phase of life, offering not only physical but also mental and social benefits. This chapter aims to guide UK pensioners through a journey of discovery of sports activities and wellness practices that can enrich their daily lives, promoting optimal health and a higher quality of life.

The Importance of Physical Activity

Several studies have demonstrated the importance of regular physical activity in preserving both mental and physical health, particularly as people age. Exercise can lower your risk of developing chronic illnesses including heart disease, type 2 diabetes, and some types of cancer, according to the NHS. It also helps maintain mobility and balance, preventing falls and improving overall quality of life.

Sports Suitable for Pensioners

There are many sports that are particularly suitable for pensioners, offering a balance between physical challenge and safety. Among them, swimming is highly recommended for its low impact on joints, while golf offers moderate activity and an opportunity for socializing. Tennis and pickleball are also gaining popularity among the elderly for their ability to improve coordination and endurance without requiring excessive exertion.

Wellness programmes

In addition to sports, wellness programmes including yoga, pilates and meditation are essential for maintaining mental and physical balance. These exercises lessen tension and anxiety while enhancing mental clarity, physical stamina, and flexibility. Specifically, mindfulness is an effective strategy for reducing everyday stress and enhancing the quality of sleep.

Food and Nutrition

Another crucial aspect of well-being is nutrition. During retirement, it is important to maintain a balanced diet that provides all the nutrients needed to support an active lifestyle. This chapter will offer advice on how to follow a diet rich in fruit, vegetables, lean protein and whole grains, and discuss the importance of hydration and moderation of alcohol consumption.

Mental Health and Socialization

Mental health is closely linked to physical health. Participating in sports groups or community activities can prevent social isolation, a risk factor for depression among the elderly. In addition, maintaining an active social network and participating in group events and hobbies can provide a sense of purpose and belonging.

Tips for getting started

For those who have never participated in sports or wellness activities, getting started may seem daunting. However, it is important to remember that it is never too late to start. This chapter will offer practical tips on how to start gradually, set realistic goals and find activities that are fun and motivating.

Testimonials and Success Stories

To inspire and motivate readers, we will include testimonials from other retirees who have transformed their lives through sport and wellness. These stories will show that with commitment and determination, it is possible to live a full and active life even after retirement.

Sport and wellness are key components of a happy and healthy retirement. By exploring different physical activities and wellness practices, retirees can improve their health, discover new passions and build meaningful relationships. This chapter will provide all the information needed to begin this journey, offering practical advice, motivation and inspiration to embrace an active and rewarding lifestyle.

Walking and Hiking: Trails and National Parks

Walking and hiking are an excellent form of physical activity and wellness, particularly suitable for retirees who wish to combine exercise and contact with nature. The UK offers a wide range of trails and national parks that are ideal for exploring the landscape and improving one's physical and mental health. This text will explore some of the best walking and hiking options in England, highlighting the opportunities they offer.

England's National Parks: Oases of Nature and Wellbeing

England is dotted with national parks offering breathtaking scenery and trails suitable for all levels of fitness. The most well-known is the Cumbrian Lake District National Park. The lakes, mountains, and undulating slopes of this park are its main draws. Walks in the Lake District vary from easy lakeside routes, such as the Tarn Hows trail, to more challenging routes offering spectacular views, such as those on Scafell Pike, England's highest mountain. For beginners, the Buttermere Trail is particularly suitable, offering a flat walk with magnificent views without too much elevation gain.

Another popular national park is the Peak District National Park, which stretches between the counties of Derbyshire, Cheshire, Staffordshire and Yorkshire. This park is known for its hilly landscapes and picturesque villages. The Dovedale Trail, famous for its spectacular limestone formations and natural bridges, is ideal for a relaxing walk. The trail is well signposted and offers opportunities to see local wildlife, making it perfect for a peaceful walk in nature.

The Yorkshire Dales National Park is another gem, with its landscapes of rolling hills and deep valleys. The Malham Cove trail is particularly impressive, with its impressive limestone arch and nearby waterfalls. This trail offers a relatively easy walk, but with breathtaking views and the chance to observe local wildlife, such as Dale's sheep.

Trails and Paths Suitable for All

Many national parks and trails in England are designed to be accessible to people of all ages and fitness levels. Paved paths and flat trails are particularly suitable for retired people or those who are returning to physical activity. For example, the Wimpole Estate in Cambridgeshire offers easy trails through beautiful gardens and farmland. Similarly, Richmond Park in London, one of the city's royal parks, offers relaxing walks through wide green spaces and the chance to observe wild deer in an urban environment.

Benefits for Health and Quality of Life

Walking in nature not only provides an excellent form of exercise, but also offers numerous mental health benefits. Research shows that spending time outdoors can reduce stress, improve mood and increase overall well-being. Walking in natural environments also helps maintain mobility and balance, which are key factors for healthy living in old age.

In addition, exploring national parks and trails offers the opportunity to socialize, which is crucial for emotional well-being. Many trails are frequented by walking groups and local organizations that offer regular events and meetings, allowing for new friendships and shared experiences.

Walking and hiking in England's national parks is an excellent opportunity to combine exercise and natural beauty. With a wide range of trails suitable for all fitness levels and numerous physical and mental health benefits, these trails offer a rewarding and sustainable way to stay active and enjoy the natural world. Whether it's a leisurely stroll along a lake or a short hike through a picturesque valley, England's national parks are ready to welcome retirees seeking wellness and adventure.

Golf: The Best Courses in the UK

Golf is a sport that combines elegance and challenge and is an excellent choice for retirees seeking a moderate but stimulating physical activity. With its many world-class courses, the UK offers outstanding opportunities for golf enthusiasts of all levels. In this text, we explore some of the best golf courses in the UK, each with their own unique characteristics that make them ideal for an unforgettable round.

1. St Andrews - Old Course

Unquestionably one of the most recognizable and storied golf courses in the world is the Old Course at St Andrews. Often regarded as the birthplace of golf, it is situated in St Andrews, Scotland. With a history dating back to 1552, this course is famous for its unique features, such as the large sand dunes and gales that can affect play. The 18-hole course winds through the coastal landscape, offering spectacular views of the sea and the ancient ruins of St Andrews Cathedral. Although playing the Old Course may require advance booking and a certain amount of luck, the experience of playing on one of the world's most prestigious courses is priceless.

2. Royal County Down

Located in Newcastle, Northern Ireland, Royal County Down is renowned for its breathtaking beauty and the challenges it presents to golfers. This course, designed by Old Tom Morris and opened in 1889, is set in spectacular scenery at the foot of the Mourne Mountains, with panoramic views of the Irish Sea. Royal County Down features undulating terrain, deep bunkers and impenetrable rough, challenging even the most experienced golfers. The course has hosted numerous prestigious tournaments, including the Walker Cup and the British Masters, cementing its reputation as one of the best golf courses in the world.

3. Royal Birkdale

Royal Birkdale Golf Club, located in Southport, England, is renowned for its challenging course and world-class quality. The course, designed by James Braid and opened in 1889, is known for its strong winds and links features, which require precise strategy and skill in play. Royal Birkdale has hosted numerous Open Championships, proving its importance in the professional golf scene. The course features wide fairways, well-placed bunkers and fast greens, offering a fascinating and rewarding challenge for golfers of all levels.

4. Royal Aberdeen

Located in Aberdeen, Scotland, Royal Aberdeen Golf Club is the second oldest golf course in Scotland, with origins dating back to 1780. The course, designed by Tom Morris and subsequently renovated, is known for its links course that stretches along the North Sea coastline. Royal Aberdeen offers a combination of traditional challenges and modern design elements, with undulating fairways, strategic bunkers and well-protected greens. This course has hosted numerous major tournaments, including the Scottish Open, and continues to be a favorite among golfers around the world.

5. Wentworth Club

For those seeking a more exclusive and luxurious golf experience, the Wentworth Club, located at Virginia Water in Surrey, is an excellent choice. This private course, designed by Harry Colt and opened in 1926, is known for its elegant setting and three golf courses, with the West Course being the most prestigious. Wentworth hosts the BMW PGA Championship, one of the most important tournaments on the European Tour, and offers a challenging course with deep bunkers, lakes and fast greens. The club also offers excellent facilities, including an elegant clubhouse and high-quality restaurants, making the playing experience even more memorable.

Some of the most renowned and captivating golf courses in the world may be found in the United Kingdom. Whether facing the challenges of the historic Old Course at St Andrews, taking in the breathtaking scenery of Royal County Down, or playing on a world-class course like Royal Birkdale, each course offers a unique and rewarding experience. For the retired golf enthusiast, these courses not only offer an excellent opportunity for exercise, but also the chance to immerse oneself in the history and beauty of British golf, creating memories that will last a lifetime.

Water Activities: Boating, Fishing and Sailing

Water activities offer a wonderful opportunity to combine exercise, relaxation and contact with nature. Whether rowing, fishing or sailing, these activities not only enrich the lives of those who enjoy them, but also promote optimal health and mental well-being. We explore each of these activities in the UK context, highlighting their characteristics, benefits and opportunities.

<u>Rowing: A Complete and Relaxing Exercise</u>

Rowing is an excellent physical activity that offers a complete, low-impact workout, ideal for those looking to keep fit without stressing their joints. The sport can be practiced on rivers, lakes and canals, and is perfectly suited to all ages and fitness levels.

In England, the River Thames is one of the most popular places for rowing. The calm waters and picturesque landscape offer a pleasant and rejuvenating experience. Rowing clubs along the Thames, such as the Leander Club in Henley-on-Thames, offer equipment and programmes for all levels, from beginners to experts.

In the north, the Lake District is another excellent destination. Lakes such as Windermere and Derwentwater offer ideal conditions for boating, with calm waters and breathtaking views. In these locations, rental centers and rowing schools provide courses and support for beginners and those who want to perfect their technique.

<u>Fishing: Relaxation and Contact with Nature</u>

Fishing is an activity that combines relaxation, patience and a deep connection with nature. Whether freshwater or sea fishing, this activity offers a quiet break from hectic life and the opportunity to enjoy the beauty of natural landscapes.

The UK is full of excellent places for fishing. The River Test in Hampshire is renowned for trout fishing and offers a peaceful and picturesque setting. This area is famous for its elegant waterways and fishing traditions.

For those who prefer sea fishing, Cornwall is an ideal destination. Outstanding boat and shoreline fishing is a well-known feature of the

Newquay region. Shore fishing, in particular, offers the chance to catch a variety of marine species, while boat trips can lead to deeper and more adventurous fishing.

Sailing: Adventure and Sense of Freedom

Sailing is an activity that combines exercise with the thrill of adventure. Sailing requires skill and coordination, but it also offers a great sense of freedom and connection with the marine environment.

The UK offers many excellent locations for sailing. The Solent, located between the Isle of Wight and the Hampshire coast, is one of the most popular sailing locations in England. This area is well known for its regattas and favorable wind conditions, making it ideal for sailors of all levels. Clubs such as the Royal Yacht Squadron offer courses and charters for beginners and experienced sailors.

Scotland is also an exceptional sailing destination. The Hebrides and the Firth of Clyde offer spectacular scenery and a network of islands and bays that can be explored by sailing. The wild beauty of the Scottish coastline and the calm waters of the bays offer a unique and unforgettable sailing experience.

Benefits of Water Activities

Water activities offer a wide range of health benefits. Rowing is an excellent cardiovascular and muscle toning exercise. Fishing, although less physically demanding, promotes relaxation and meditation. Finally, sailing is an activity that combines physical exercise with improved problem-solving and coordination skills.

Moreover, all these activities promote contact with nature, which has been proven to have positive effects on mental health and general well-being. Spending time outdoors, in natural and peaceful settings, can reduce stress, improve mood and offer a sense of fulfilment and joy.

Boating, fishing and sailing are water activities that offer not only excellent exercise but also an opportunity to enjoy the natural beauty of the UK.

Whether paddling down a serene river, embarking on a day of fishing or surfing the waves with a sailboat, these activities can enrich lives and promote lasting well-being. With a wide range of locations and opportunities available, there is something for everyone looking to explore the aquatic world and improve their quality of life.

Yoga and Meditation: Physical and Mental Wellbeing

Yoga and meditation are age-old practices that offer profound benefits for both body and mind. These disciplines not only promote physical well-being, but also contribute to greater mental serenity and a more balanced life. In this text, we will explore in detail how yoga and meditation can enrich lives, especially in old age, and offer practical suggestions for integrating these practices into daily routines.

Physical Benefits of Yoga

Yoga is an age-old discipline that incorporates meditation, controlled breathing (pranayama), and physical postures (asanas). Yoga poses are very helpful for senior citizens since they enhance strength, flexibility, and balance. Asanas help maintain joint mobility and strengthen muscles without over-stressing the joints, thus reducing the risk of injury and improving the quality of daily life.

Gentle or gentle yoga postures, such as baby posture (Balasana) and cat posture (Marjaryasana), are ideal for beginners and those seeking a more relaxed practice. These exercises help maintain correct posture and prevent muscular pain, which is often caused by being sedentary.

In addition, regular yoga practice can improve blood circulation and digestion, and promote more restful sleep. Improved breathing and reduced stress contribute to better overall health.

Mental Benefits of Meditation

Meditation is a practice that involves concentration and awareness and can be particularly helpful in managing stress and anxiety. Various meditation techniques, such as mindfulness meditation, breath control and mindfulness meditation, can help calm the mind and develop greater inner clarity.

For instance, mindfulness meditation promotes accepting thoughts and feelings without passing judgement and concentrating on the here and now. This method lessens tension and enhances one's capacity to handle challenges in daily life. The regular practice of meditation can also improve memory and concentration, crucial factors in maintaining an active and lively mind as we age.

<u>Integrating Yoga and Meditation into Daily Life</u>

Integrating yoga and meditation into daily life does not necessarily require a large amount of time. The general state of well-being can be greatly impacted by even brief daily sessions. The following useful advice can help you incorporate these habits into your daily routine:

Establish a Routine: Set aside some time each day to meditate and practise yoga. A just 10 to 15 minutes daily can have a significant impact. Pick a time of day that works for you and provides you with uninterrupted concentration.

Create a Quiet Space: Find a corner of the house that can be dedicated to your practice. A quiet, well-lit area, perhaps with a yoga mat and meditation cushions, can create an environment conducive to practice.

Start with Videos and Apps: There are numerous online resources, including videos and apps, that guide you through yoga and meditation sessions. Those who like a step-by-step guide and are beginners may find these to be especially helpful.

Participate in Group Classes: Yoga and meditation classes are widely available in many places, both in person and online. Enrolling in these courses can offer encouragement, inspiration, and a sense of community.

Be Consistent: The key to lasting benefits is consistency. Although it may be difficult at first, maintaining a regular practice helps to integrate yoga and meditation as part of your daily routine.

Particularly in later life, yoga and meditation are effective practices for enhancing both mental and physical health. These exercises not only enhance mental clarity and stress reduction, but also flexibility, strength, and balance. With just a few minutes a day devoted to these practices, significant improvements in health and quality of life can be achieved. A happier, more balanced, and more satisfying life can result from including yoga and meditation into your everyday routine.

Introduction to birdwatching and nature reserves in the UK

Birdwatching, or bird watching, is an activity that combines the pleasure of exploring nature with the fascinating study of different avian species. This activity is particularly popular in the UK, which boasts an extraordinary variety of habitats and nature reserves, offering numerous opportunities to spot a wide range of birds in the wild. Whether you are an experienced ornithologist or a curious beginner, birdwatching can be a highly rewarding experience, enriching your knowledge of nature and offering moments of tranquility and wonder.

The Fascination of Birdwatching

Birdwatching is more than just a pastime; it is an activity that promotes environmental awareness and a deep respect for biodiversity. Observing birds in their natural habitat requires patience, attention to detail and a keen eye, qualities that help develop a deeper connection with the surrounding environment. Each sighting can be an exciting discovery, stimulating curiosity and continuous learning about different species and their behaviour.

In the UK, birdwatching can be practiced in any season of the year, as the country is inhabited by a rich variety of resident and migratory species. In spring and autumn, the skies are filled with migratory birds crossing the country, offering breathtaking natural spectacles. Summer brings with it the song of nesting birds, while winter offers the opportunity to spot rare species that find refuge in the more temperate parts of the UK.

UK Nature Reserves

The UK's nature reserves are veritable birdwatching havens. These protected places provide ideal habitats for a multitude of avian species, ensuring the conservation of biodiversity and offering birdwatchers the opportunity to spot birds in pristine environments. Here are some of the most important and impressive nature reserves in the country:

RSPB Minsmere (Suffolk): Managed by the Royal Society for the Protection of Birds (RSPB), Minsmere is one of the most famous reserves in the UK. Located on the east coast of England, it offers a variety of habitats, including lagoons, marshes, woodlands and beaches. Species such as bitterns, ospreys and shrikes can be spotted here.

Bempton Cliffs (Yorkshire): This coastal reserve is renowned for its spectacular cliffs, which are home to one of the largest seabird colonies in the UK. Between April and July, the cliffs are animated by thousands of puffins, magpies, gannets and guillemots, providing an extraordinary natural spectacle.

Skomer Island (Wales): Located off the coast of Pembrokeshire, Skomer Island is an island rich in wildlife. It is famous for its colony of puffins and numerous seabirds, including three-toed gulls and cormorants. The island is accessible during the summer season and offers a unique birdwatching experience.

The Farne Islands (Northumberland): A group of islands located off the north-east coast of England, the Farne Islands are a sanctuary for numerous species of seabirds and seals. Sightings include Arctic terns, puffins and tufted plovers.

Loch Garten (Scotland): Located in the heart of the Cairngorms National Park, Loch Garten is famous for its population of ospreys. During spring and summer, visitors can observe these magnificent birds of prey as they nest and raise their young. The reserve also offers opportunities to spot crossbills and redwing thrushes.

Preparing for birdwatching

To get started with birdwatching, it is useful to have some essential tools. To observe birds up close without upsetting them, you'll need good binoculars, and a UK bird guide can assist you distinguish between different species. Also, dressing appropriately for the weather conditions and carrying a bottle of water and some snacks can make the experience more enjoyable.

Birdwatching is an activity that requires patience and silence. Finding a good vantage point, staying still and paying attention to sounds and movements can increase the chances of interesting sightings. Taking notes and photos can help document observations and share the experience with other enthusiasts.

Birdwatching in the UK is an exciting activity that offers a deep connection with nature and the chance to explore some of the country's most beautiful landscapes. Nature reserves provide safe habitats for many bird species and ideal places to observe them. Whether you are a beginner or an expert, birdwatching can enrich your life with moments of wonder and serenity, while promoting the conservation of our precious biodiversity.

Birdwatching Equipment: My Personal Guide

Birdwatching has become one of my greatest passions in recent years. The feeling of watching birds in their natural habitat is indescribable, and over time I have learnt that having the right equipment can make a big difference. I would like to talk to you about my experiences. After spending many hours in various habitats, I have realized how important it is to have the right equipment to make the experience more enjoyable and productive. Here is a list of the essential tools I always carry with me and some tips on how to use them to best effect.

Binoculars

A good pair of binoculars is probably the most important tool for any birdwatcher. My favorite binoculars are those with 8x42 magnification.

The number 8 refers to the magnification, while 42 is the lens diameter in millimetres. These types of binoculars offer a good balance between magnification and image brightness, making them ideal for observations in different light conditions. It is important to choose a model that is light and has good ergonomics so that it can be held comfortably even for prolonged periods.

Notebook and Pencils

I always carry a notebook and some pencils with me. Jotting down observations is essential to improve my identification skills and to remember the most significant sightings. I record the date, time, place, weather conditions and a detailed description of the birds I see. This helps me create a personal archive and note changes in migratory habits or local populations.

Birdwatching guide

A good birdwatching guide is indispensable. I prefer versions with detailed illustrations and information on bird distribution, behavior and song. When I am in the field, I use a pocket guide that allows me to quickly compare what I see with the descriptions in the book. There are also many smartphone apps that offer interactive functions, such as bird song recognition, that can be very useful.

Camera

If you love photography, as I do, a camera is a must. I use a digital SLR with a telezoom lens (preferably 300mm or more) to capture close-up images without disturbing the birds. Make sure you have a large memory card and spare batteries. Photographing birds is not only a way to preserve memories, but also a useful tool for identifying difficult species once back home.

Appropriate clothing

Clothing can make a big difference. I always wear comfortable, layered clothes to adapt to changes in the weather. I prefer neutral or camouflage colors so as not to frighten the birds. Shoes must be sturdy and waterproof, especially when walking on rough or wet terrain. A hat and sunscreen are essential to protect me from the sun, while a light mackintosh keeps me dry in case of rain.

Backpack

A sturdy rucksack is necessary to transport all the gear. Not too large, yet large enough to accommodate everything I need. I prefer a rucksack with lots of pockets to organize my equipment and with a holder for my binoculars so that I always have them to hand. I also usually have a first aid kit, energy snacks, and a bottle of water with me.

Field Telescope

For more detailed observations, especially over long distances, I use a field telescope. This instrument is particularly useful in coastal areas or reserves where birds may be far away. It takes a strong tripod to maintain the image's stability. Although it is bulkier to carry than binoculars, the telescope offers an unparalleled level of detail.

Gloves and Hand Warmers

During winter outings, gloves are essential to keep your hands warm, especially when holding binoculars or writing in the notebook. I use thin gloves that allow me to have a good sense of touch. Hand warmers are useful to add a little extra warmth on colder days.

With the right equipment, birdwatching becomes an even more rewarding activity. Every outing is an adventure and a new opportunity to learn and discover. Remember, the key is to be prepared and patient: nature always rewards those who observe carefully and respectfully.

Benefits of forest walks and suggested routes

Forest walks offer a rejuvenating and immersive experience that combines physical exercise with direct contact with nature. This simple and accessible activity is a great way to improve physical and mental health while promoting general well-being. Exploring forest trails allows one to discover the beauty and tranquility of nature, offering a refuge from the hustle and bustle of everyday life. In this text, we will explore the benefits of woodland walks and suggest some ideal routes in the UK to make the most of this activity.

Physical Benefits of Woodland Walking

Walking in the woods is an excellent cardiovascular exercise that helps to keep the heart healthy and improve circulation. The uneven terrain of forest paths offers an additional challenge compared to flat surfaces, stimulating different muscle groups, improving balance and increasing leg and core strength. In addition, regular walks help maintain a healthy weight, reduce the risk of chronic diseases such as type 2 diabetes and hypertension, and improve bone density.

Mental and Emotional Benefits

Spending time in the woods has been shown to have significant positive effects on mental health. The natural world fosters serenity and tranquilly by lowering stress and anxiety levels. Immersion in nature has been demonstrated in scientific research to reduce cortisol levels, a stress hormone, and enhance mood. In addition, walking in the woods stimulates the production of endorphins, contributing to a feeling of well-being and happiness. Connecting with nature also promotes increased alertness and concentration, making forest walks an excellent remedy for burnout and mental fatigue.

Social benefits

Forest walks can also be a social activity, providing an opportunity to spend quality time with friends and family. Walking together strengthens social bonds, facilitates communication and creates shared memories. In addition, joining walking groups or hiking clubs can help you meet new people with similar interests, expanding your social network and creating a sense of community.

Suggested routes in the UK

The UK is full of beautiful woodlands and forests that offer ideal walking routes. Here are some of the best places to immerse yourself in nature:

New Forest, Hampshire: This ancient royal forest is a true nature lover's paradise. With its wide paths, ancient oak and beech trees, and varied wildlife, the New Forest offers numerous trails suitable for all ages and fitness levels. One suggested route is the Bolderwood Deer Sanctuary Walk, where you can spot free-roaming deer.

Sherwood Forest, Nottinghamshire: Famous for the Robin Hood legend, Sherwood Forest is a fascinating place for a walk. The Major Oak Trail is a popular route that leads to the famous Major Oak, a tree over 800 years old that is said to have been the refuge of Robin Hood and his companions.

Epping Forest, London: Located a short distance from the center of London, Epping Forest offers a green and peaceful retreat. With over 2,400 hectares of ancient woodland, this forest is perfect for a rejuvenating walk. The Connaught Water Circular Walk is an easy, scenic route around a picturesque lake.

Grizedale Forest, Lake District: Nestled in the heart of the Lake District, Grizedale Forest is renowned for its breathtaking scenery and outdoor sculptures. The Ridding Wood Trail is an enchanting route that combines nature and art, leading through dense woodland and panoramic views.

Kielder Forest, Northumberland: The Kielder Forest is the largest man-made forest in England, offering an extensive network of trails to choose from. The Lakeside Way is a circular trail that follows the perimeter of Kielder Water, the largest man-made lake in the UK, offering beautiful views of the water and surrounding forest.

Woodland walks are an easy and enjoyable way to improve physical and mental health while enjoying the beauty of nature. The benefits of this activity are many, and the UK offers a wide range of routes suitable for all levels of experience. Whether it is a solitary walk to reflect and relax, or a group outing to socialize and share the wonder of nature, woodland walks are a deeply life-enriching and lasting activity.

Chapter 5 Volunteering Opportunities

Volunteering is one of the most rewarding and meaningful experiences a person can have. Not only does it offer the chance to contribute positively to the community, but it also enriches the lives of those who engage in such activities with a sense of purpose and fulfilment. For retired people, volunteering can be an unmissable opportunity to find new energy and motivation, making a valuable contribution as you explore a new chapter in your life.

In the chapter on volunteering opportunities, we will explore how and why volunteering can be an excellent choice for retirees, illustrating the many ways in which you can help and make a difference. From participating in community projects to supporting non-profit organizations, the options are wide and varied, allowing you to find the activity that best suits your passions and skills.

The Value of Volunteering in the Third Age

Volunteering is not only a form of helping others, but also extremely beneficial for those who practice it. For pensioners, it can be a way to maintain an active and involved lifestyle. Research shows that engaging in voluntary activities is associated with numerous health benefits, including increased life satisfaction, reduced risk of depression and improved general well-being. Through volunteering, it is possible to stay socially connected, learn new skills and feel an integral part of the community.

Furthermore, volunteering offers a unique opportunity to continue using and developing one's professional and personal skills, contributing to projects and causes that are important and meaningful. Whether teaching, offering practical support or leading local initiatives, the contribution of an experienced volunteer can have a profound and lasting impact.

Diversity of Volunteering Opportunities

Volunteering opportunities are extremely diverse and can cater for a wide range of interests and abilities. This chapter will explore some of the main categories of volunteering:

Community Volunteering: Many retirees choose to dedicate their time to local projects, such as running food banks, participating in support groups or organizing community events. These roles not only help solve immediate needs, but also help build social bonds and promote a sense of cohesion in the community.

Volunteering for Non-Profit Organizations: Non-profit organizations offer a wide range of opportunities for volunteers, from administrative tasks to field work. Whether it is an organization that supports scientific research, environmental protection or human rights, retirees can find a role that aligns with their passions and skills.

Mentoring and Tutoring: Many retirees have a wealth of experience and knowledge that can be shared with younger generations. Mentoring and tutoring programmes offer the opportunity to mentor and coach emerging students and professionals, helping to shape the next generation and making a lasting impact.

Online Volunteering: With the rise of digital resources, online volunteering has become an increasingly popular modality. This type of volunteering allows people to contribute to global projects without the need for physical travel, making it particularly accessible to those with mobility limitations or who prefer to work from home.

How to start

To start volunteering, it is essential to identify your passions and interests. Assessing the type of work, you would like to do and the causes you would like to support is the first step. In addition, many organizations offer orientation sessions and trial opportunities to help new volunteers better understand what their role entails and how they can make a difference.

In this chapter, we will also provide practical tips on how to find volunteering opportunities, how to contact local organizations, and how to prepare for a volunteering role. We will also offer inspiring stories of retirees who have found meaning and satisfaction through volunteering, demonstrating the positive impact these activities can have on both the community and personal life.

Volunteering is a powerful and rewarding way for retirees to stay active, involved and fulfilled. With a wide range of opportunities available, it is possible to find an activity that not only fulfils one's passions but also makes a significant contribution to society. This chapter guides the reader through the world of volunteering, providing an overview of the opportunities and benefits, and encouraging them to discover the invaluable value of dedicating time and skills to an important cause.

Contributing to the Community: Organizations and Associations

Contributing to the community is an activity that enriches not only those who receive help, but also those who offer their time and skills. Being part of voluntary organizations and associations allows you to create meaningful bonds, develop new skills and feel an integral part of your community. In the UK, there are many organizations and associations that offer volunteering opportunities in various areas, from supporting the vulnerable to protecting the environment. In this text we explore some of these organizations and the value of volunteering to the community and to individuals.

Social Volunteering

Social volunteering is one of the most widespread and important sectors. It involves activities that support people in need, such as the elderly, the disabled, refugees and the homeless. Here are some of the main organizations working in this field:

Age UK: This organization is dedicated to improving the quality of life for older people. Volunteers can participate in telephone companionship programmes, home visits, recreational activities and support in daily errands. These activities help combat loneliness and promote the social inclusion of older people.

Shelter: Shelter works to address homelessness and precarious housing conditions. Volunteers can offer administrative support, participate in awareness-raising campaigns and provide legal advice. By making a donation to Shelter, you can ensure that everyone has access to a respectable and safe place to live.

Refugee Action: This group assists refugees and those applying for asylum in the United Kingdom. Volunteers can help with English language teaching, orientation in the local community and legal support. These activities facilitate the integration of refugees and improve their life chances.

Environmental Volunteering

Another important aspect of environmental conservation and protection is environmental volunteering. Numerous organizations are devoted to this goal:

The Wildlife Trusts: The preservation of animals and natural ecosystems is the main goal of this network of regional organizations. Volunteers can participate in wildlife monitoring projects, nature site management and educational programmes. These activities help protect biodiversity and promote environmental awareness.

National Trust: The National Trust preserves historic places and natural landscapes throughout the UK. Volunteers can help maintain gardens, trails and historic properties, as well as participate in events and educational activities. These initiatives preserve cultural and natural heritage for future generations.

Friends of the Earth: This environmental organization focuses on awareness-raising campaigns and direct action to tackle problems such as climate change, pollution and biodiversity loss. Volunteers can participate in campaigns, petition drives and public awareness activities. These actions help create a more sustainable future.

Cultural and Recreational Volunteering

Cultural and recreational volunteering involves activities that enrich the cultural and social life of the community:

Museums Association: Many museums and galleries in the UK offer volunteering opportunities. Volunteers can help as guides, exhibition assistants and participate in educational programmes. These activities promote culture and arts education.

Sport England: This organization promotes sport and physical activity. Volunteers can help organize sports events, coach youth teams and participate in sports inclusion programmes. Sports volunteering improves the health and well-being of the community.

Local Community Centres: Local community centers offer a variety of recreational and cultural programmes. Volunteers can organize courses, events and activities for all ages, fostering social cohesion and providing opportunities for learning and fun.

Benefits of Volunteering

Volunteering not only enriches the community, but also offers numerous benefits to the volunteers themselves. Participating in volunteer activities allows them to develop new skills, gain practical experience and improve their communication and leadership skills. In addition, volunteering promotes mental wellbeing, reduces stress and increases personal satisfaction. Feeling useful and making a difference in the lives of others is one of the most rewarding experiences one can have.

Contributing to the community through volunteering is an act of generosity that has a profound and lasting impact. Organizations and associations in the UK offer a wide range of opportunities to help those in need, protect the environment and enrich the cultural life of the community. Participating in these initiatives not only improves society, but also enriches the lives of volunteers, creating meaningful bonds and fostering a sense of belonging and personal fulfilment.

Volunteering in Hospitals and Nursing Homes

Volunteering in hospitals and nursing homes is an activity that can have a profoundly positive impact on both the patients and the volunteers themselves. These care environments require support and assistance to improve the quality of life of elderly people and patients, often coping with illness, loneliness or the natural ageing process. Here is how volunteering can make a difference and some of the main activities in which volunteers can be involved.

Benefits of Volunteering for Patients and the Elderly

Volunteering in these settings offers numerous benefits. Patients and elderly people in nursing homes often experience loneliness and social isolation. The presence of volunteers can alleviate these feelings by providing companionship and emotional support. Regular social interactions can improve their mood, reduce anxiety and promote a sense of belonging and personal value.

In addition, volunteers can contribute to the physical well-being of residents and patients through activities that promote mobility and light exercise. Even small daily interactions, such as walks or board games, can have a positive effect on their physical and mental health.

Benefits of Volunteering

Volunteering in hospitals and nursing homes is not only beneficial for the recipients, but also offers many advantages to the volunteers. This may be a very fulfilling and enriching experience that gives you a sense of purpose and fulfilment. Volunteers develop new skills, such as empathic communication, patience and understanding the needs of others.

In addition, volunteering in these environments can provide valuable practical experience for those wishing to pursue a career in health care, social work or psychology. Even those who do not seek a career in these areas may find that volunteering improves their personal and social well-being, reducing their stress and increasing their self-esteem.

Volunteering in Hospitals

Emotional Support and Companionship: Volunteers can spend time with patients, listen to their stories, read books aloud or simply chat. These interactions help combat loneliness and offer comfort.

Assisting with Daily Activities: Volunteers can help with practical tasks such as accompanying patients to internal medical examinations, helping with meals or providing support during walking.

Organization of Recreational Activities: Volunteers can organize and participate in various recreational activities such as board games, creative workshops, music therapy and reading sessions. These activities provide fun and mental stimulation.

Administrative Support: Some volunteers may help with administrative tasks, such as welcoming visitors, handling bookings or assisting with documentation.

Voluntary Activities in Nursing Homes

Companionship programmes: Many elderly people in old people's homes do not receive frequent visits. Volunteers can offer them company, listening to their stories, sharing hobbies or simply spending time together.

Assistance with Recreational Activities: Volunteers can organize activities such as light exercise, gardening, arts and crafts, board games and film screenings. These activities keep older people active and engaged.

Support in Daily Care: Although volunteers do not replace medical staff, they can provide assistance with daily activities such as dressing, eating and mobility, improving the quality of life of older people.

Intergenerational Interactions: Some nursing homes organize programmes involving young volunteers. These intergenerational interactions can be very enriching for both parties, promoting cultural and social exchanges.

How to Start

For those interested in becoming a volunteer in hospitals or nursing homes, the first step is to contact local organizations and find out about available opportunities. Most organizations require volunteers to complete a short training period to ensure that they are prepared to perform their tasks effectively and safely. In addition, background checks may need to be passed to ensure the safety and well-being of patients and elderly people.

Volunteering in hospitals and nursing homes is a deeply meaningful activity that offers tangible benefits to both recipients and volunteers. Through companionship, practical support and participation in various activities, volunteers can improve the quality of life of patients and elderly people, while contributing to their own personal development and emotional well-being. This experience enriches the community, promoting values of empathy, solidarity and altruism.

Environmental and Conservation Projects

Involvement in environmental and conservation projects is a unique opportunity to contribute to the protection and improvement of our planet. These projects are crucial for the preservation of biodiversity, the fight against climate change and the promotion of sustainable development. Participating in such initiatives not only helps the environment, but also offers the chance to acquire new skills, meet people with similar interests and have meaningful experiences. In this text, we will explore the benefits of environmental and conservation projects and provide examples of initiatives in the UK.

Benefits of Environmental and Conservation Projects

Participating in environmental and conservation projects offers numerous benefits. Firstly, it directly contributes to the protection of the natural environment. Planting trees, cleaning up beaches, monitoring wildlife and restoring natural habitats are just some of the activities that can have a tangible positive impact on the local and global ecosystem.

In addition, these projects offer a unique learning opportunity. Volunteers can gain in-depth knowledge about local flora and fauna, conservation practices and environmental management techniques. These skills can be useful both for those who wish to pursue a career in the environmental sector and for those who simply want to enrich their personal culture.

Examples of Environmental and Conservation Projects in the UK

The Wildlife Trusts: This network of local organizations is committed to the conservation of wildlife and natural habitats throughout the UK.

Projects include grassland restoration, creation of ecological corridors, monitoring of endangered species and environmental education. Volunteers can take part in a variety of activities, such as managing nature sites and observing birds.

The Woodland Trust: The goal of the Woodland Trust is to preserve and restore natural woodlands. Projects include planting trees, restoring ancient forests and promoting forest biodiversity. Volunteers can help by planting trees, removing invasive species and participating in public awareness events.

Marine Conservation Society (MCS): MCS focuses on protecting the UK's oceans and coastline. Projects include cleaning beaches, monitoring sea turtle populations and promoting sustainable fishing. Volunteers can participate in marine litter collection campaigns, environmental education programmes and scientific research.

National Trust: The National Trust protects and preserves historic sites and natural landscapes. Environmental projects include the management of nature reserves, the conservation of rare habitats and the promotion of sustainable tourism. Volunteers can help with trail maintenance, invasive species management and organizing educational events.

RSPB (Royal Society for the Protection of Birds): The RSPB is the largest nature conservation organization in the UK, dedicated to the protection of birds and their habitats. Projects include establishing nature reserves, monitoring bird populations and promoting biodiversity conservation. Volunteers can participate in bird censuses, habitat restoration activities and educational programmes.

How to get started

For those interested in participating in environmental and conservation projects, the first step is to identify local organizations working in your area. Visiting the websites of these organizations and contacting them directly to find out about available volunteer opportunities is a great way to get started. Many organizations offer training sessions to prepare volunteers for specific activities, ensuring that they are well equipped to contribute effectively.

Participating in environmental and conservation projects is a meaningful way to make a difference and contribute to the health of our planet. These projects not only help protect and restore natural ecosystems, but also provide opportunities for learning, personal development and community connection. Through environmental volunteering, we can all contribute to a more sustainable and prosperous future for future generations.

Chapter 6 Continuous Learning

Retirement represents a time of great change in a person's life. After decades dedicated to working and building a career, old age offers the opportunity to explore new passions and interests that may have been put aside during working years. One of the most rewarding and beneficial activities during this phase of life is continuous learning. This chapter aims to explore the many learning opportunities available to older people, highlighting the cognitive, emotional and social benefits of keeping the mind active and curious.

The Value of Lifelong Learning

Education shouldn't be restricted to a single life stage. Numerous benefits of constant learning for mental and physical health have been demonstrated by scientific investigations. It maintains mental activity, enhancing cognitive and memory functions. In addition, learning new skills and knowledge can increase self-esteem and a sense of personal fulfilment.

Moreover, continuous learning is a powerful antidote against boredom and loneliness, common problems in old age. Participating in courses, seminars or study groups offers the opportunity to socialize and create new friendships, reducing the risk of social isolation and depression.

Learning Opportunities

Learning opportunities for older people are vast and varied. Senior universities, online courses, creative workshops and study groups are just some of the options available. These platforms offer courses on an incredibly wide range of topics, from art history to science, from literature to technology.

Universities of the Third Age (U3A): Universities of the Third Age are organizations that offer courses and educational activities for senior citizens. These courses are often taught by volunteers who are experts in various fields and cover a wide range of topics. The U3A promotes learning without the pressure of examinations, allowing seniors to explore their passions in a relaxed and friendly environment.

Online Courses: Technology has opened new doors for continuous learning. Platforms such as Coursera, edX and FutureLearn offer free or low-cost online courses on a wide range of topics. These courses, often created by prestigious universities and institutions, allow seniors to learn from the comfort of their own home and at their own pace.

Creative Workshops and Practical Courses: For those who prefer more hands-on learning, creative workshops and practical courses are an excellent option. Whether painting, photography, cooking or gardening, these activities allow you to develop new manual and artistic skills. In addition, participating in creative workshops is an excellent way to socialize and share common interests with other people.

Reading Groups and Book Clubs: Reading groups and book clubs offer a wonderful opportunity to explore literature and discuss one's opinions and interpretations with other book lovers. These groups promote intellectual debate and social interaction, enriching the reading experience.

Cognitive and Emotional Benefits

The benefits of ongoing education extend to mental and emotional health. It lowers the risk of dementia and cognitive decline by stimulating and activating the mind. Learning new skills and knowledge can also increase brain plasticity, improving the brain's ability to adapt and change.

Emotionally, continuous learning provides a sense of purpose and fulfilment. Acquiring new skills and gaining new knowledge can increase self-esteem and self-confidence. In addition, the social interaction that results from participation in courses and study groups can reduce loneliness and improve emotional well-being.

Continuous learning in old age is an invaluable practice that enriches the lives of older people in many ways. It offers a way to keep the mind active, acquire new skills, socialize and find a sense of purpose. Through the many learning opportunities available, older people can continue to grow and develop, living a full and rewarding life. This chapter will explore these opportunities in detail, providing practical tips and inspiration for embracing lifelong learning in old age.

Online Courses and Universities of the Third Age

Continuous learning in old age represents a valuable opportunity to enrich one's life, keep one's mind active and socialize. Two of the most accessible and flexible options for older people are online courses and Universities of the Third Age (U3A). Both of these modes of learning offer numerous advantages and cater for the different needs and interests of older people.

Online Courses

In recent years, access to online courses has become increasingly easy, thanks to a wide range of educational platforms available. These courses offer unparalleled flexibility, allowing seniors to learn new topics from the comfort of their own home and at their own pace.

Educational Platforms: Some of the most popular platforms include Coursera, edX, FutureLearn and Udemy. These platforms collaborate with prestigious universities and educational institutions to offer high-quality courses on a wide range of topics, from history and literature to science and technology.

Accessibility: Online courses are often free or available at a reduced cost. Many courses also offer the possibility of obtaining official certificates by paying a small fee. This affordability makes lifelong learning accessible to all, regardless of financial resources.

Variety of Content: The variety of courses available online is extraordinary. Seniors can choose from thousands of courses according to their personal interests, whether academic, practical or personal development. This allows them to explore new fields or deepen already acquired knowledge.

Learning Communities: Many online courses include discussion forums and virtual study groups where students can interact, ask questions and share experiences. These virtual communities offer a valuable opportunity to socialize and exchange ideas.

Universities of the Third Age (U3A)

Universities of the Third Age are organizations that offer courses and educational activities specifically designed for older people. These universities are based on the principle of self-learning and knowledge sharing, without the pressure of examinations and assessments.

Structure of U3As: U3As are generally local organizations run by volunteers. They offer a wide range of courses taught by other senior or experienced volunteers. These courses cover a multitude of topics, including history, foreign languages, social sciences, arts, music and much more.

Collaborative Learning: One of the fundamental principles of U3A is collaborative learning. Students actively share their knowledge and experiences rather than only being passive consumers of it. This method encourages an engaging and dynamic learning environment.

Social Benefits: U3A offers an important opportunity for socialization. A sense of community and belonging is fostered by seniors who share interests in classes and activities. In this setting, friendships have the potential to be deeply profound and enduring.

Complementary Activities: In addition to academic courses, many U3As offer complementary activities such as excursions, cultural events, creative workshops and discussion groups. These activities further enrich the educational experience and provide opportunities for recreation and fun.

Comparison of Online Courses and U3A

Both online courses and U3A offer unique advantages. Online courses are ideal for those seeking flexibility and access to a wide range of topics from anywhere. U3As, on the other hand, offer a more social and collaborative experience, with the opportunity to interact face-to-face with other seniors.

Continuous learning in old age is an excellent way to keep the mind active, acquire new skills and build meaningful relationships. Whether through online courses or Universities of the Third Age, older people have numerous resources at their disposal to explore new interests and enrich their lives. Regardless of the method chosen, the important thing is to keep learning and growing, finding joy and satisfaction in learning for a lifetime.

Reading and Discussion Clubs

Reading and discussion clubs provide a valuable opportunity to keep the mind active, stimulate intellectual curiosity and create meaningful social connections. These clubs provide an environment for older people to share the pleasure of reading, deepen their understanding of texts and exchange views with other book lovers. Participating in a book club can be an enriching and rewarding experience in many ways. In this text, we will explore the benefits of these clubs, how they work, and how to start or find a suitable book club.

Benefits of Reading and Discussion Clubs

Participating in a book club offers numerous benefits, both intellectually and socially. First of all, reading regularly and discussing books helps to keep the mind active and stimulated. Analyzing texts, understanding complex topics and critical thinking are activities that improve cognitive skills and memory.

In addition, book clubs foster socialization and the building of new friendships. Discussing books in a group creates a sense of community and offers the opportunity to meet people with similar interests. This can reduce the sense of isolation and loneliness common in old age and improve emotional well-being.

How Reading and Discussion Clubs Work

Reading clubs can vary widely in how they are organized and how they meet, but they generally follow a common structure:

Selection of Books: Club members choose books to read together. This choice can be democratic, with voting on a list of suggestions, or it can be delegated to a club coordinator. The variety of genres and authors chosen can enrich the reading experience.

Frequency of Meetings: Reading clubs usually meet once a month, giving members sufficient time to read the selected book. Meetings can take place in different locations, such as libraries, cafes, private homes or even online.

Discussion: During the meetings, members discuss the book they have read. Discussions can follow a free structure or be guided by questions prepared in advance. This moment of confrontation allows for exploring different points of view and deepening the understanding of the text.

Social Aspects: In addition to literary discussion, book club meetings can include social moments, such as dinners or tea, which further foster socialization and a sense of community.

How to Start or Find a Reading Club

If you would like to join a book club or start one, here are some suggestions:

- Local Search: Many libraries, bookshops and community centers organize reading clubs. Enquire with these institutions to find out if there are reading clubs in your area.
- Online platforms: Virtual and local reading clubs can be found on a variety of websites. Meetup, Goodreads and Facebook are good starting points to search for reading groups.
- Start a club: If you cannot find a suitable reading club, consider starting one. Recruit friends, family members or neighbours interested in reading. Choose a meeting place and establish a schedule for meetings. Remember to maintain an inclusive and welcoming atmosphere.
- Bookshops and Libraries: Some bookshops and libraries offer meeting spaces and can help promote your book club. Collaborating with these institutions can increase the visibility of your club and attract new members.

Reading and discussion clubs offer an extraordinary opportunity for older people to keep their minds active, explore new literary horizons and build meaningful relationships. Through shared reading and in-depth discussions, members of these clubs can enrich their intellectual and social lives. Whether you choose to join an existing club or create your own, participating in a book club can bring joy, intellectual stimulation and new friendships. The important thing is to cultivate a passion for reading and to share this experience with others.

Museums and Galleries: Subscriptions and Guided Tours

Museums and galleries are ideal places to explore culture, art and history, and offer valuable opportunities to stimulate the mind and enrich life in old age. Visits to these institutions can be particularly rewarding thanks to two ways of participating: subscriptions and guided tours. Both offer unique advantages, allowing one to discover permanent collections and temporary exhibitions, and can be adapted to different personal interests and preferences. This text will explore the benefits and opportunities offered by subscriptions and guided tours, offering practical advice on how to get the most out of these cultural experiences.

Museum and Gallery Subscriptions

Museum and gallery subscriptions are an excellent option for those who wish to visit these places frequently and enjoy exclusive benefits.

Economic advantages: A season ticket allows unlimited visits to museums and galleries for a period of time, usually one year. This is especially advantageous for those who like to explore different exhibitions or return to exhibitions already visited. Often, a subscription can be cheaper than buying single tickets, especially if you plan to visit frequently.

Early and Exclusive Access: Many museums offer season ticket holders early access to special exhibitions or exclusive events. This may include private evenings, early openings or meetings with curators and artists, offering a more intimate and in-depth experience.

Discounts and Special Offers: Subscriptions often include discounts on items in the museum shop, restaurants and cafés. Some museums also offer additional benefits, such as discounts on tickets to affiliated shows and cultural events.

Notifications and Updates: Subscription holders receive regular newsletters and updates on upcoming exhibitions, events and educational programmes. This allows them to stay informed and plan visits in advance.

Guided Visits

Guided tours offer a unique opportunity to explore museums and galleries with the assistance of experts and guides, enriching the cultural experience with insights and context that might be missed during a stand-alone visit.

Insight and Context: Expert guides provide detailed information about the artworks, artists and collections. This helps to better understand the meaning and history of the exhibitions, enhancing the visitor experience.

Thematic Experiences: Many museums offer thematic guided tours that focus on specific aspects of the collection or on particular topics, such as the art of a certain historical period or an artistic technique. These specialized tours can deepen specific aspects and enrich the visitor's understanding.

Interaction and Questions: Guided tours allow visitors to ask questions and interact directly with the guide. This can be particularly useful for clarifying doubts, exploring topics of personal interest and deepening aspects that are not immediately apparent.

Group and Customized Tours: Many museums offer guided tours for private groups, which can be customized according to the interests of the group. This is particularly advantageous for groups of friends or associations that wish to explore a collection together, creating a shared and socializing experience.

How to Choose and Use Subscriptions and Guided Tours

Research and Registration: In order to choose the most suitable subscription, it is useful to visit the museums' websites or contact them directly. Check the benefits included costs and renewal options. For guided tours, check the calendar of events and book in advance to secure a place, especially for themed visits or popular exhibitions.

Planning Visits: Use the information provided by newsletters and updates to plan your visits. If you have a subscription, make the most of the flexibility offered to explore different exhibitions and return to your favorite routes.

Active Participation: During guided tours, actively participate in discussions and take advantage of opportunities to ask questions. This will allow you to make the most of the experience and enrich your knowledge.

Museum and gallery subscriptions, together with guided tours, offer a wide range of opportunities to explore and appreciate culture and art. Whether you choose to invest in a subscription for unlimited access or participate in guided tours for in-depth understanding, these experiences can greatly enrich your life. With the right planning and participation, museums and galleries can become places of continuous learning and personal discovery, making each visit a stimulating and rewarding adventure.

Participate in British history or genealogy courses to discover your roots

Discovering one's roots and understanding the history of one's family and country is a profound and enriching experience that can bring new perspectives and meaning to one's life. Participating in British history or genealogy courses offers older people a unique opportunity to explore the past, connect with their roots and gain a deeper understanding of their cultural and family roots. This text will explore the benefits of such courses, how to participate and how to get the most out of these educational experiences.

Benefits of British History and Genealogy Courses

Connecting with the Past: British History courses offer a detailed overview of the events, figures and dynamics that have shaped the United Kingdom over the centuries. Knowing your country's history not only enriches your understanding of the historical and cultural context, but also creates a sense of connection and belonging.

Discovering Family Roots: Genealogy courses focus on the study of one's family origins. By researching archives, records and historical documents, one can trace one's ancestry and discover hidden family histories and connections. This process not only reveals fascinating details about one's roots but can also create a sense of identity and continuity.

Intellectual stimulation: Enrolling in courses on history and genealogy promotes critical thinking and mental stimulation. Analyzing historical sources and genealogical documents requires attention to detail and research skills, keeping the mind active and engaged.

Socialization and Community: Enrolling in classes on history and genealogy gives the chance to connect with individuals who share your interests. Study groups and class discussions can lead to new friendships and a social support network, enriching the learning experience.

How to Participate in Courses

University and Academic Courses: Many universities and academic institutions offer courses in British history and genealogy. These courses can vary in duration and level of depth, from short seminars to diploma programmes. Enrolling in university courses can provide a structured, high-quality education.

Online Courses: Online education platforms such as Coursera, edX and FutureLearn offer British history and genealogy courses that can be taken from the comfort of home. Flexible and independent study is made possible by the inclusion of reading materials, discussion boards, and video lectures in these courses.

Local and Community Courses: Many libraries, community centers and local associations organize history and genealogy courses. These courses can be more informal and community-oriented, offering an opportunity to learn in a convivial and accessible environment.

Workshops and Workshops: Workshops and hands-on workshops are another way of learning. These events can focus on specific genealogical research techniques, such as using genealogy software or consulting historical archives. Attending such events provides an opportunity to apply the skills acquired and obtain practical assistance.

How to Make the Most of History and Genealogy Courses

Set Clear Objectives: Before starting a course, it is useful to set clear objectives on what you want to achieve. Whether it's deepening your knowledge of British history or charting your own genealogy, having specific goals helps focus learning and measure progress.

Participate Actively: Getting actively involved in discussions and course projects enhances the learning experience. Asking questions, sharing personal discoveries and participating in group activities enriches understanding and promotes deeper learning.

Using Additional Resources: Taking advantage of additional resources such as books, articles, online archives and research tools can expand knowledge and provide additional information. Local libraries and historical archives can offer valuable resources for genealogical research.

Documenting and Sharing Discoveries: Documenting the results of genealogical research and the knowledge gained can be rewarding. Creating family trees, writing family histories or organizing information in a visible format can help preserve and share discoveries with family and friends.

Taking British history and genealogy courses is an excellent way to explore your roots and enrich your knowledge of the past. These courses not only offer a stimulating learning opportunity, but also foster a connection to one's cultural and family heritage. Whether you choose university, online, local or workshop courses, the important thing is to take advantage of these experiences to discover, understand and celebrate your personal and national history.

Genealogy Courses

In England, there are several courses and training programmes dedicated to genealogy that can help you discover and deepen your family history.

Here are some renowned courses and institutions that offer excellent learning opportunities in genealogy:

1. The University of Strathclyde - Master of Science in Genealogical, Palaeographic and Heraldic Studies

The Master's course offered by the University of Strathclyde is one of the most comprehensive and prestigious in the field of genealogy and historical research. It focuses on advanced aspects of genealogy, such as paleography (the study of ancient manuscripts) and heraldry (the study of coats of arms). It is a full-time or part-time course, suitable for those who wish to pursue a professional career in genealogy or to seriously deepen their skills.

Website: University of Strathclyde - MSc Genealogical, Palaeographic and Heraldic Studies

2. The National Archives - Genealogy Courses

The National Archives offers a variety of courses and workshops on genealogy. These courses are designed to help researchers navigate archives and historical resources, making the most of the historical records available for genealogical research. Courses cover topics such as researching archives, using online resources and managing genealogical data.

Website: The National Archives - Learning

3. Family History Federation - Certificate in Family History Research

The Family History Federation (FHF) offers a Certificate in Family History Research that is highly respected in the field of genealogy. This course is designed to help participants develop the skills needed to conduct in-depth genealogical research. The course covers various aspects of research, including the use of civil and ecclesiastical records, and genealogical analysis techniques.

Website: Family History Federation - Certificate in Family History Research

4. The Society of Genealogists - Courses and Workshops

The Society of Genealogists offers a range of courses and workshops on various aspects of genealogy. These include introductory courses for beginners, as well as more advanced workshops on specific topics such as the use of military records, online resources and research techniques. The Society of Genealogists is one of the UK's leading genealogical organizations and also offers consultancy services and research resources.

Website: Society of Genealogists - Courses and Workshops

5. University of London - Postgraduate Certificate in Genealogy, Palaeography and Heraldic Studies

Offered through the Institute of Historical Research, this postgraduate certificate focuses on specialized aspects of genealogy, including paleography and heraldry. It is suitable for those wishing to further their genealogical skills and pursue a career or advanced interest in the field.

Website: University of London - Postgraduate Certificate in Genealogy, Palaeography and Heraldic Studies

6. Ancestry Academy - Online Genealogy Courses

Numerous online courses covering a broad range of genealogy topics are available at Ancestry Academy. Advanced research methods, internet resource utilisation, and analytic tools are all covered in these courses. They are designed to help researchers get the most out of Ancestry resources and improve their genealogy skills.

Website: Ancestry Academy - Genealogy Courses

7. The Genealogical Society of Utah (FamilySearch) - Online Courses

FamilySearch, part of the Genealogical Society of Utah, offers a number of free online courses and educational resources. These courses cover various aspects of genealogy, from introduction to research to compiling family trees, and are accessible to anyone, anywhere.

Website: FamilySearch Learning Centre

Participating in these courses will provide you with valuable tools and knowledge to explore your family history and deepen your understanding of genealogy. Whether you are a beginner or an experienced researcher, there are options for all levels of experience and interest.

Lessons in foreign languages or music to stimulate the mind

Investing time in learning a new language or deepening musical skills is an excellent way to stimulate the mind and enrich life in old age. Both of these areas offer numerous cognitive, emotional and social benefits, helping to keep the mind active, improve communication skills and promote general well-being. This text will explore in detail how foreign language lessons and music can stimulate the mind and improve quality of life.

Benefits of Foreign Language Lessons

Cognitive Stimulation: Learning a new language is an excellent exercise for the brain. Research has shown that language learning can improve memory, attention and problem-solving skills. The process of learning new grammatical structures and vocabulary stimulates neuronal connections and can help keep the brain agile and healthy.

Improved Communication Skills: Knowing more languages allows you to communicate with people from different cultures and backgrounds, expanding opportunities for socialization. This can lead to new friendships and meaningful interactions, enriching one's social life and providing a sense of global connectedness.

Increased Self-Confidence: Gaining confidence might come from learning a new language. Being able to communicate in another language allows one to travel, experience new things, and grow personally. Every small success in language learning contributes to a greater sense of achievement and self-esteem.

Prevention of Cognitive Decline: Language learning has been associated with a delay in the onset of neurodegenerative diseases such as

Alzheimer's. Continuous cognitive activity, such as that required for language learning, can help keep the brain healthy and resilient.

Ways of Learning Languages

Formal courses: Many universities and educational centers offer foreign language courses for adults. These courses are structured and often include classroom lectures, practical exercises and study materials. Formal courses provide a solid foundation and a clear path for learning.

Private Lessons: For individuals who desire individualised attention, private sessions can be a flexible choice. A private teacher can tailor lessons to the student's specific interests and needs, facilitating more focused and in-depth learning.

Apps and Online Resources: Platforms such as Duolingo, Babbel and Rosetta Stone offer online language courses accessible at any time. These apps and websites are useful for learning new vocabulary and phrases through interactive exercises and games.

Conversation Groups: Participating in language conversation groups can improve practical skills and provide real practice opportunities. These groups, often organized by cultural centers or associations, provide an informal environment to practice the language and socialize.

Benefits of Music Lessons

Improved Memory and Concentration: Learning to play a musical instrument or sing can improve memory and concentration. Music stimulates different areas of the brain involved in auditory processing, memory and motor coordination, helping to keep the mind active and agile.

Emotional Expression and Stress Reduction: Music offers a powerful means to express emotions and reduce stress. Playing an instrument or singing can serve as therapy and relaxation, improving mood and providing a way to express feelings in a healthy and creative way.

Development of Social Skills: Joining a chorus or taking group music classes offers chances to interact and work together with people. This can promote a sense of community and belonging by resulting in more social interactions and new connections.

Maintaining Coordination and Motor Skills: Playing a musical instrument requires coordination and fine motor control, which can help maintain motor skills and dexterity as they age.

Music Learning Modalities

Private Instrument Lessons: Private lessons for piano, guitar, violin and other instruments are a popular choice. An experienced teacher can tailor lessons to the student's level and interests, providing customized training.

Group Courses: Group music courses, such as choirs or bands, offer an opportunity to learn together with others. These courses foster socialization and can be very rewarding for those who enjoy group interaction.

Apps and Online Resources: Apps such as Yousician and Simply Piano offer interactive music lessons that can be followed at home. These resources provide tools for learning and practicing music independently and flexibly.

Workshops and Seminars: Participating in music workshops and seminars can provide an intensive, hands-on experience with the opportunity to learn new techniques and improve one's musical skills in a short period of time.

Participating in foreign language or music lessons is an excellent way to stimulate the mind and enrich one's life during old age. These activities offer numerous cognitive and social benefits, helping to keep the brain active, improve communication skills and promote emotional well-being. Whether you choose to learn a new language or play a musical instrument, these experiences can offer joy, personal growth and meaningful new connections.

Chapter 7 Social and Group Activities

Throughout life, social and group activities play a crucial role in maintaining emotional well-being and a sense of belonging. This is especially true during old age, a time when people may face significant changes such as retirement, loss of friends or family, and transition to new stages of life. Participating in social and group activities not only helps maintain a connection with others, but also provides valuable opportunities to continue growing, learning, and having fun. In this chapter, we will explore how social and group activities can enrich the lives of those in retirement, contributing to improving the quality of life and promoting active and fulfilling ageing.

Social and group activities, ranging from local clubs and associations to cultural and recreational activities, offer numerous benefits. Participating in these events helps counter social isolation, a common problem among older people that can lead to feelings of loneliness and depression. Instead, being part of a group can provide a sense of community and belonging, improve mental and physical health, and offer new perspectives and experiences.

The Benefits of Social and Group Activities

Improved Mental Health: Social and group activities are essential for maintaining mental health. Regular interaction with other people helps prevent loneliness and reduce the risk of depression and anxiety. Conversations, mutual support and shared experiences can alleviate feelings of isolation and promote a positive, healthy mind.

Intellectual stimulation: participating in discussion groups, book clubs or thematic courses stimulates the mind and promotes continuous learning. These activities provide opportunities to explore new interests, acquire knowledge and remain mentally active, contributing to improved memory and cognitive skills.

Improving Social Skills: Group activities provide an ideal context for developing and maintaining social skills. Interacting with other group members, participating in discussions and working together on common projects improves communication and collaboration skills, making it easier to make new friends and build strong social networks.

Opportunities for Fun and Relaxation: Participating in social and group activities should not only be productive, but also enjoyable. Social events, parties, and recreational activities offer moments of fun and relaxation, allowing one to enjoy the company of others and relax in a positive and stimulating environment.

Types of Social and Group Activities

Local Clubs and Associations: Local clubs and associations are excellent starting points for those seeking social activities. These groups often focus on common interests such as reading, cooking, gardening, or crafts, providing a welcoming environment to connect with others who share similar passions.

Volunteer Groups: Volunteering is a form of social participation that not only helps others, but also offers a sense of purpose and personal satisfaction. Volunteer groups can include activities such as supporting animal shelters, distributing food, or mentoring young people. These experiences enrich lives and foster a sense of community.

Cultural and Recreational Activities: Cultural activities, such as attending plays, concerts, or art exhibitions, provide stimulating and enriching experiences. Participating in art, dance or music classes can also be a fun and creative way to interact with others and discover new passions.

Community events: community events such as fairs, markets, and local celebrations provide opportunities to meet people and have new experiences. Engaging in these activities can enhance one's feeling of community and foster a lively, welcoming social atmosphere.

Social and group activities are essential for a full and satisfying life in old age. They offer not only mental and physical health benefits, but also opportunities to grow, have fun and make meaningful connections with others. This chapter will provide insights into how to explore and participate in different social and group activities, helping you integrate these experiences into your daily life and enjoy the many benefits they offer. Connecting with others and staying active and involved is essential for healthy and happy ageing.

Clubs and Societies: Joining Groups with Common Interests

Joining clubs and societies with common interests is one of the most rewarding ways to enrich one's social and personal life, especially during old age. These groups offer a stimulating environment where one can connect with people who share similar passions and interests, thus helping to improve emotional well-being, foster the development of new skills and maintain a vibrant social life. In this text, we explore how clubs and societies can transform your life, offering numerous benefits and suggesting ways to find and participate in groups that reflect your interests.

Benefits of Joining Clubs and Societies

Socialization and a Sense of Belonging: Participating in a club or society allows you to meet people with similar interests, fostering socialization and creating new friendships. A sense of belonging to a group helps combat loneliness and isolation, which can be problematic during old age. Sharing common activities and goals helps build lasting and meaningful bonds.

Intellectual stimulation and personal growth: clubs and societies often offer opportunities to learn new skills and deepen knowledge in specific areas. Whether it is a reading club, a hiking group or a photography society, organized activities stimulate the mind and promote personal growth. Participation in events, workshops and discussions helps to keep the brain active and engaged.

Support and Sharing: Groups provide an important support system. In times of difficulty or change, having a network of people who understand your passions and challenges can offer comfort and motivation. Sharing experiences and listening to each other strengthens the sense of community and solidarity.

Volunteering and Civic Engagement Opportunities: Many clubs and societies are engaged in volunteer activities and community improvement projects. Participating in these initiatives offers the chance to make a positive contribution to society and to feel part of something bigger. This commitment can enrich lives and provide a feeling of fulfilment and purpose.

Types of Clubs and Societies

Reading Clubs: Reading clubs are ideal for those who love books and wish to discuss their reading with other enthusiasts. These groups meet regularly to talk about novels, essays and other texts, providing a space to explore new readings and share opinions.

Outdoor Activity Clubs: If you enjoy being outdoors, consider joining a hiking, cycling or birdwatching club. These groups organize hikes, walks and outdoor activities, allowing you to enjoy nature, stay active and meet people with similar interests.

Art and Culture Societies: Art and culture societies, such as theatre, photography or painting groups, offer opportunities to express creativity and participate in cultural events. These groups organize exhibitions, performances and workshops, providing opportunities to develop talents and share artistic passions.

Hobby and Interest Clubs: From gardening clubs to cooking groups, clubs based on specific hobbies are a great way to meet people who share your interests. Participating in these activities allows you to deepen personal passions and acquire new skills.

Volunteer societies: Many organizations offer volunteer opportunities in different areas, such as social work, environmental protection and supporting local communities. These societies not only allow you to contribute to the common good, but also to make new acquaintances and feel part of a support network.

How to Find and Join Clubs and Societies

Search Online: Using social media and websites, a large number of groups and organizations are present online. To locate local groups and societies that share your interests, use social media and search engines.

Local Notice Boards and Announcements: Community centers, libraries and local universities often post announcements about events and groups. Check the notice boards and ask for information at these venues to discover opportunities in your area.

Networking Events: Attend local events, fairs and networking meetings to discover new groups and meet members. These events offer a chance to make acquaintances and find clubs that align with your interests.

Recommendations and Word of mouth: Find out whether your friends, relatives, and acquaintances are aware of any intriguing organizations. Personal recommendations can guide you to clubs and societies that might be particularly suitable for you.

Joining clubs and societies with common interests is an excellent way to enrich one's social and personal life. They offer opportunities to socialize, learn new skills, receive support and contribute to the community. Whether it is a book club, an outdoor activity group or a volunteer society, these groups can provide a sense of belonging and enrich lives in meaningful ways. Investing time and effort in these activities will help you live a fuller, more rewarding and connected life.

Local Events and Fairs

Participating in local events and fairs is a vibrant and rewarding way to connect with your community, discover new opportunities and enrich your social life. These events offer a variety of experiences ranging from culture and art to food and local traditions, creating unique opportunities to socialize, learn and have fun. This text will explore how and why taking part in local events and fairs can be extremely beneficial and will provide tips on how to find and participate in these activities.

Benefits of Attending Local Events and Fairs

Strengthening the Sense of Community: Participating in local events helps you feel an integral part of your community. These events celebrate local traditions and cultures, allowing you to learn more about your city and its inhabitants. Interacting with neighbours and participating in local celebrations reinforces a sense of belonging and helps create meaningful social bonds.

Socializing Opportunities: Local events and fairs are excellent opportunities to meet new people and make friends. Meeting others with similar interests or simply sharing experiences in a festive or cultural context can lead to new connections and relationships. These events often attract a variety of participants, offering opportunities to expand one's social network.

Exploring New Experiences: local fairs and events offer a wide range of experiences, from art exhibitions to culinary tastings, from historical events to sports competitions. Participating in these events allows one to discover and try new things, which can enrich one's life and stimulate interests and passions. It is also an excellent way to stay up to date with the latest news and trends in your area.

Supporting the Local Economy: Participating in local fairs and events often involves supporting small businesses and local artisans. Local manufacturers and companies can showcase their goods and services on these occasions. Buying from local vendors and participating in community events helps to strengthen the economy of one's area and support local initiatives.

Mental Stimulation and Entertainment: The variety of activities and entertainment available during local fairs and events provides mental stimulation and entertainment. Participation in workshops, shows, and interactive activities helps keep the mind active and provides moments of leisure and pleasure.

How to Find and Attend Local Events and Fairs

Consult Local Calendars and Websites: Many cities and municipalities have online calendars listing upcoming events and fairs. These calendars are often available on the websites of local governments, cultural centers or community forums. Keeping an eye on these sites can help you discover interesting events and plan your participation.

Subscribe to Newsletters and Interest Groups: Many local events have newsletters or social media groups through which they send out updates and information. Subscribing to these newsletters or following these groups on platforms such as Facebook can provide you with timely information about upcoming events and allow you to stay informed about activities in your area.

Visit Community Centres and Libraries: Community centers and local libraries often have notice boards and information material about events and fairs. These places are also great for getting recommendations and suggestions on what to do in your area.

Attend Networking Events: Networking events and local meetings can offer opportunities to discover new events and meet people who are already involved in community activities. These meetings often offer useful information and contacts for attending events and fairs.

Asking Local Residents: Talking to friends, family and acquaintances who live in your area can provide valuable advice on local events and fairs. Personal recommendations can guide you to activities that may not be widely publicized but are particularly appreciated by the community.

Participating in local events and fairs offers a wealth of benefits ranging from strengthening a sense of community to discovering new experiences and socializing with others. These events not only provide opportunities to have fun and learn, but also to support the local economy and keep cultural traditions alive. Investing time in attending local fairs and events can greatly enrich your life, providing memorable experiences and meaningful connections in your community. With careful planning and an open curiosity, you can discover and enjoy the wonders your area has to offer.

List of Local Events and Fairs

Here is a list of some of the most important local events and fairs in the UK, ranging from cultural and historical celebrations to food and art events. These gatherings provide special chances to learn about British culture and establish connections with the locals.

Important Events and Fairs in the UK

<u>Cultural and Historical Events</u>

The Edinburgh Festival Fringe (Edinburgh, Scotland) - August

The biggest and most well-known arts event in the world is the Edinburgh event Fringe. Every August, the city hosts a wide range of theatre, comedy, music and dance performances in hundreds of different venues.

The London Marathon (London, England) - April

One of the most prestigious marathons in the world, the London Marathon attracts runners and spectators from all over the globe. The event is also known to raise significant funds for charity.

The Royal Edinburgh Military Tattoo (Edinburgh, Scotland) - August

This military and musical spectacle takes place annually at Edinburgh Castle. With performances by military bands, dancing and drama, it is one of the most spectacular events of the summer festival.

Glastonbury Festival (Glastonbury, England) - June

Considered one of the most iconic and widely recognized music festivals in the world, Glastonbury presents a line-up of international artists and a wide range of cultural and artistic events.

The Notting Hill Carnival (London, England) - August

This lively festival celebrates Caribbean culture with colorful float parades, reggae, soca and calypso music, and a wide selection of traditional food and drink.

Gastronomic Events

The Great British Food Festival (Various locations in England) - Dates variable

This food fair celebrates British food with stalls from local producers, tastings and cooking demonstrations.

The BBC Good Food Show (Birmingham, England) - November

This annual food event, organized by the BBC, features celebrity chefs, food and drink producers, and a wide range of gourmet products.

The Oxford Cheese Festival (Oxford, England) - November

An event dedicated to cheese lovers, offering tastings of artisan and local cheeses, along with educational events and family activities.

Art and Design Events

London Design Festival (London, England) - September

This festival celebrates design and architecture with exhibitions, events and installations across London, attracting designers and enthusiasts from all over the world.

The Chelsea Flower Show (London, England) - May

One of the world's most prestigious gardening exhibitions, the Chelsea Flower Show presents beautiful gardens and flower arrangements.

The Manchester International Festival (Manchester, England) - July

A biennial festival presenting new works of visual art, music, theatre and dance, with a focus on experimentation and artistic innovation.

Historical and Traditional Events

Hampton Court Palace Flower Show (London, England) - July

The UK's second largest garden show, held at Hampton Court Palace and featuring inspirational gardens and floral displays.

The Hay Festival (Hay-on-Wye, Wales) - May/June

A literary festival that brings together authors, readers and intellectuals for discussions and readings. Hay-on-Wye is known as the 'city of books' and hosts this annual event with a wide range of cultural programmes.

The Yorkshire Show (Harrogate, England) - July

One of the largest and oldest agricultural fairs in the UK, celebrating agriculture, food and crafts with animal displays, cooking demonstrations and family events.

The Glastonbury Abbey Extravaganza (Glastonbury, England) - August

An annual musical event held on the ancient site of Glastonbury Abbey, with performances by internationally renowned artists.

Attending local events and fairs is an excellent way to discover and enjoy the traditions and cultures of the UK. Each event offers a unique opportunity to explore personal passions, socialize and support local communities. Whether it be music festivals, food fairs, historical celebrations or art exhibitions, there is always something interesting and exciting to experience.

Organize and Participate in Group Excursions

Putting together and taking part in group outings is a great opportunity to meet new people, discover the outdoors, and create lifelong memories. Whether it is a leisurely walk in a local park or a more challenging hike in a nature reserve, group hikes offer numerous benefits, including socializing, promoting health and discovering new places. This text will explore how to organize and participate effectively in group hikes, providing practical tips and advice to ensure an enjoyable and safe experience.

Benefits of Group Excursions

Socializing and Connecting: Participating in group excursions offers the opportunity to meet people with similar interests and build new friendships. Hikes are ideal opportunities to socialize in an informal environment, exchange experiences and enjoy each other's company while exploring nature.

Motivation and Support: When participating in a group hike, collective motivation can be a great incentive. Being part of a group offers support and encouragement, making it easier to tackle longer or more challenging trails and maintain a steady pace.

Health and Well-being: Hiking is excellent for improving physical and mental health. Walking outdoors and spending time in nature encourages physical activity, reduces stress and improves general well-being. Participating in a group hike can make these activities more enjoyable and rewarding.

Discovery of New Places: Group hikes can lead you to discover places you might not otherwise visit. Groups often explore lesser-known trails or areas of natural beauty that might not be easily accessible on their own, offering new and enriching experiences.

How to Organize a Group Excursion

Planning and Preparation: The first step in organizing a group excursion is planning. Decide on the date and time of the hike, choose a route that suits the participants' abilities and interests, and make sure the route is safe and well signposted. It is useful to consult maps and local resources to gather detailed information on the route and conditions.

Communication and Invitations: Once you have planned the hike, send out invitations to participants with all the necessary information, such as departure time, meeting point and route details. Use communication platforms such as e-mail, social media groups or messaging apps to keep everyone informed and up to date.

Equipment preparation: Make sure all participants are prepared for the hike. Advise them to wear comfortable clothing and suitable shoes, and to bring water, snacks, sunscreen and a waterproof jacket if the weather is uncertain. Also bring a map of the route and a first aid kit for possible emergencies.

Safety and Responsibility: Safety is paramount during a group hike. Establishing some basic rules, such as keeping the group together and respecting personal boundaries, helps to ensure that everyone feels safe. Designate a responsible person to supervise the group and ensure that everyone is aware of emergency points and procedures in case of accidents.

Organization of the hike: During the hike, lead the group so that everyone can enjoy the experience. Maintain a pace that allows everyone to participate and encourage regular breaks for rest and refreshment. Take advantage of stops to share information about the route and points of interest, making the outing more educational and engaging.

How to Participate in Group Excursions

Be Punctual and Prepared: Arrive on time and prepared for the hike. As directed by the coordinator, ensure that you have all the necessary materials for the activity.

Be Collaborative and Flexible: Being part of a group requires collaboration and flexibility. Honour the decisions made by the group and add something constructive to the experience as a whole. Maintain a positive attitude and encourage other participants.

Follow Rules and Guidelines: Adopt safe and responsible behavior by following the rules set by the excursion coordinator. Respect nature and other people, keeping the trail clean and orderly.

Be Inquisitive and Active: Seize the chance to investigate and acquire knowledge. Engage fully in conversations and activities with the group and make an effort to meet new people while on the walk.

Organizing and participating in group excursions is an excellent way to socialize, improve health and discover new places. Careful planning and active participation ensure that the outing is safe, fun and memorable for all participants. Whether an informal stroll or a more challenging hike, group outings offer rich and rewarding experiences that can enrich your life and the lives of others.

Chapter 8 Luxury Travel and Unique Experiences

The United Kingdom, with its rich history, breathtaking landscapes and vibrant culture, offers countless opportunities for those seeking luxury travel and unique experiences. From majestic Scottish castles to elegant English country houses, from culinary adventures in cosmopolitan cities to relaxing retreats in the countryside, the UK is a perfect destination for those wishing to explore luxury in all its forms.

The Charm of Castles and Historic Houses

One of the most fascinating aspects of luxury travel in the UK is the opportunity to stay in castles and historic mansions. These buildings, often set in centuries-old parks, offer a unique experience that combines the charm of history with modern comfort. Mansions such as the Cliveden House in Berkshire or the Gleneagles Hotel in Scotland are perfect examples of how historical elegance can be combined with high-class amenities. Staying in these places is not only about enjoying luxurious accommodation, but also about immersing oneself in history, exploring immaculately manicured gardens and savoring refined dishes prepared by starred chefs.

Culinary Experiences of Excellence

The UK has become one of the world's leading culinary destinations, with a dining scene that boasts Michelin-starred restaurants and gourmet pubs. London in particular is a global culinary hotspot with a vast array of restaurants serving a variety of cuisines. Unforgettable eating experiences can be had at establishments like Heston Blumenthal's The Fat Duck, Gordon Ramsay's Restaurant, and The Ledbury. However, luxury dining experiences are not limited to the capital. Across the nation, from the Scottish Highlands to the coastal villages of Devon, you will find inns and restaurants that celebrate the best of British cuisine with fresh local ingredients.

Luxury Spa and Wellness Retreats

For those seeking the ultimate in relaxation and wellness, the UK offers some of the best luxury spas and retreats in the world. Locations such as

Champneys Health Spa and Lime Wood Hotel and Spa are renowned for their rejuvenating treatments and serene environments. These retreats offer a wide range of treatments, from traditional therapies to modern holistic treatments, all set in beautiful natural landscapes that encourage tranquility and relaxation.

Exclusive Adventures and Experiences

The UK is also a great destination for those seeking unique and exclusive adventures. From private helicopter tours over the cliffs of Dover to luxury cruises along the Thames, the possibilities are endless. Motoring enthusiasts can experience the thrill of driving an Aston Martin or Bentley through the scenic roads of the Cotswolds, while history buffs can join private tours of the country's most iconic historical sites, such as Stonehenge or Windsor Castle.

High-Profile Cultural Events

Attending high-profile cultural events is another way to experience luxury in the UK. The Chelsea Flower Show, Royal Ascot and the Edinburgh Festival are just some of the events that offer an exclusive experience, combining culture, tradition and luxury. These events not only allow you to enjoy the best cultural and sporting performances, but also to socialize with the UK's cultural and social elite.

The UK offers a wide range of luxury experiences that go far beyond five-star accommodation. Every corner of the country has something unique to offer, whether it is a stay in a castle, a dinner in a starred restaurant, a rejuvenating spa treatment or an exclusive adventure. In this chapter, we explore these experiences in detail, providing tips on how best to experience the luxury and sophistication that the UK has to offer.

Luxury Cruises: The Best Offers

Luxury cruises represent one of the most exclusive and rewarding forms of travel. They offer the perfect mix of comfort, adventure and discovery, all with the utmost relaxation and impeccable service. The United

Kingdom, with its long maritime tradition, is an ideal starting point for many luxury cruises that traverse not only British waters, but also the beautiful coastlines of Europe and other global destinations. In this text we explore some of the best luxury cruise offers available, highlighting the distinctive features of each and providing advice on how to choose the perfect cruise.

1. Cunard Line

The Cunard Line is synonymous with elegance and maritime tradition. Its iconic ships, such as the Queen Mary 2, Queen Elizabeth and Queen Victoria, offer a luxury cruise experience that combines the charm of the past with modern comforts. Cunard cruises include transatlantic itineraries, linking the UK to the US, as well as cruises exploring the Mediterranean, Norwegian fjords and the Baltic. On board, guests can enjoy spacious suites, gourmet cuisine and high-quality entertainment, as well as a wide range of cultural and social activities.

2. Silversea Cruises

Silversea Cruises is known for its small to medium-sized ships that offer personalized service and an intimate atmosphere. Silversea cruises cover a wide range of destinations, including the Mediterranean, Northern Europe, Asia and the Americas. Suites are all equipped with a personal butler, and guests can enjoy top-notch restaurants, included in the all-inclusive offer. The Silversea is also distinguished by its exclusive shore excursions, which allow guests to explore destinations in an in-depth and authentic way.

3. Regent Seven Seas Cruises

Regent Seven Seas Cruises offers an all-inclusive cruise experience of the highest standard. Its ships are all-suite, with private balconies and luxurious amenities. Regent's itineraries cover all regions of the world, with an emphasis on detail and comfort. Cruises include unlimited shore excursions, premium drinks, gratuities and Wi-Fi. On board, guests can take part in cooking classes, theatre performances and cultural programmes, all in a sophisticated and relaxed environment.

4. Seabourn Cruise Line

Seabourn Cruise Line is famous for its fleet of small luxury ships that offer highly personalized service and unique itineraries. Seabourn cruises explore exclusive destinations such as Antarctica, Alaska, Asia and the Mediterranean. The suites are spacious and tastefully furnished, and every detail is taken care of to ensure maximum comfort. Seabourn's all-inclusive offers include world-class dining, premium drinks and gratuities, as well as a personal butler service.

5. Crystal Cruises

Crystal Cruises is renowned for its excellence in service and well-equipped luxury ships. Crystal cruises offer itineraries around the world, with a strong emphasis on cultural and adventurous experiences. The ships are equipped with elegant suites, luxury spas, swimming pools and numerous gourmet restaurants. Crystal Cruises also includes high-quality shore excursions designed to offer an authentic immersion in local cultures.

Tips for Choosing the Perfect Cruise

- Destination: Consider the destinations you wish to explore. Luxury cruises offer itineraries all over the world; therefore, choose the one that best suits your travel interests.
- Services: Evaluate the services included in cruise offers. Some lines offer all-inclusive packages that cover excursions, drinks and gratuities, making your trip more relaxing and worry-free.
- Ship size: Smaller ships offer a more intimate experience and personalized service, while larger ships offer a greater variety of entertainment and activities.
- Reviews: Read reviews from other travelers to get an idea of the past experiences and strengths of each cruise line.
- Budget: Establish your spending limit and search for deals that provide the most value for your money, keeping in mind the inclusions included in the cruise fare.

Luxury cruises represent one of the most fascinating forms of travel, combining the elegance of sea transportation with exotic destinations and high-class services. Whether you are looking for an adventure through the North Seas, a cultural exploration in the Mediterranean or an excursion to the pristine waters of Antarctica, there are numerous luxury cruise options to suit every desire. With careful planning and choosing the right cruise line, you can enjoy an unforgettable experience that will allow you to discover the world in comfort and style.

Stays in Historic Hotels and Resorts

At the heart of UK culture and history, stays in historic hotels and resorts offer a unique and fascinating travel experience. These accommodations not only provide a high level of service and modern comforts, but also allow you to immerse yourself in the country's rich historical heritage. From medieval castles to Georgian mansions, each property has a story to tell, offering visitors the opportunity to live like royalty for a few days. In this text, we explore some of the UK's most prestigious historic hotels and resorts, highlighting their unique features and why they are ideal destinations for those seeking an unforgettable stay.

1. Cliveden House, Berkshire

Cliveden House is one of the most iconic resorts in the UK. Situated in Berkshire, this magnificent 17th-century mansion is encircled by 376 acres of breathtaking woodland and gardens. Over the ages, Cliveden has played home to dignitaries, presidents, and movie stars. It was initially constructed for the Duke of Buckingham. Luxurious rooms and suites with individually designed antiques and artwork are available for guest accommodations. Cliveden also offers a world-class spa, an outdoor pool and several gourmet restaurants, making it a perfect destination for relaxation and wellness.

2. The Ritz, London

The Ritz in London is synonymous with luxury and elegance. Opened in 1906, this historic hotel has retained its charm and is considered one of the most prestigious hotels in the world. Located in the heart of London, The

Ritz offers an unparalleled experience with its sumptuously appointed rooms and suites, impeccable service and the famous Afternoon Tea in the Palm Court. The hotel is also home to the renowned Michelin-starred Ritz restaurant, offering fine dining in sophisticated surroundings.

3. Gleneagles Hotel, Scotland

Nestled in the picturesque hills of Perthshire, the Gleneagles Hotel is a historic resort offering a luxurious experience surrounded by the natural beauty of Scotland. Opened in 1924, Gleneagles is famous for its three world-class golf courses, but also offers a wide range of outdoor activities, including horse riding, clay pigeon shooting and fishing. The hotel's rooms and suites combine traditional Scottish charm with modern comforts, while the resort's restaurants serve dishes prepared with fresh local ingredients.

4. Bovey Castle, Devon

Bovey Castle, located in the heart of Dartmoor National Park, is another example of a historic resort offering a luxury experience surrounded by nature. Built in the early 20th century, Bovey Castle boasts majestic architecture and opulent interiors. Guests can enjoy a wide range of activities, including golf, falconry and walks in the beautiful gardens. The resort also offers a luxury spa and award-winning restaurants serving fine cuisine.

5. Ashford Castle, Ireland

Although not located in the UK, Ashford Castle in Ireland is worthy of mention for its proximity and historical importance. This 13th century castle, located on the banks of Lough Corrib, has been transformed into a luxury hotel offering a regal experience. With its majestic towers, perfectly manicured gardens and elegantly furnished rooms, Ashford Castle is an ideal destination for those seeking a luxurious stay steeped in history.

Staying in a historic hotel or resort in the UK is a unique opportunity to experience luxury in a setting steeped in history and culture. These accommodations offer not only modern comforts and high-class services, but also a journey into the past, allowing visitors to discover the fascinating stories and personalities that shaped these mansions. Whether it is an elegant mansion in Berkshire, an iconic hotel in the heart of London or a majestic castle in Scotland, each property offers a unique and unforgettable experience. Choosing one of these historic hotels for your stay means not only enjoying the ultimate in luxury, but also immersing yourself in the history and culture of the United Kingdom.

Gourmet Experiences: Gastronomic Tours and Tastings

Gourmet experiences have become a major attraction for travelers seeking culinary adventures. The UK, with its rich gastronomic tradition and culinary innovation, offers a wide range of gourmet tours and tastings that will delight the most discerning palates. From London to the Scottish countryside, exploring the UK's gastronomic offerings is a journey that combines culture, history and unforgettable flavors. In this text, we explore some of the best gourmet experiences available, highlighting tours and tastings that offer total immersion into the world of British cuisine.

1. London Gourmet Tours

London is one of the world's most diverse capitals, and this diversity is reflected in its culinary scene. London food tours provide an opportunity to sample traditional foods, explore local markets, and learn about the newest trends in cooking. An excellent place to start is Borough Market, one of the city's most well-known and historic food marketplaces. Here, visitors can sample a wide range of fresh produce, from artisanal cheeses to cured meats and freshly prepared gourmet dishes.

Another point of interest is the tour of London's historic pubs. This tour allows you to discover some of the city's oldest and most characteristic pubs, sampling local beers and traditional dishes such as fish and chips and pies. For those looking for something a little more exclusive, London's Michelin-starred restaurants offer unique tasting experiences, with tasting menus created by the world's best chefs.

2. Whisky Tasting in Scotland

Scotland is famous for its whisky, and a visit to local distilleries is a must for fans of this drink. Distillery tours offer the opportunity to see the whisky production process, from raw materials to distillation and ageing. The Speyside region, known as the whisky capital of Scotland, is home to some of the most prestigious distilleries, such as Glenfiddich and Macallan. Here, visitors can participate in guided tours and tastings that include rare and long-aged whiskies.

Another region not to be missed is the Isle of Islay, famous for its peaty whiskies. Distilleries such as Laphroaig, Ardbeg and Lagavulin offer immersive experiences, with tastings directly from the casks and the chance to create your own whisky blend.

3. Vineyard tours in England

In recent years, England has emerged as a successful wine region, with sparkling wines competing internationally. Vineyard tours in the south of England offer the opportunity to explore wineries, learn about viticulture techniques and taste a selection of award-winning wines. The Kent region, often called the 'Garden of England', is home to a number of wineries, including Chapel Down and Gusbourne, which offer guided tours and tastings.

4. Culinary Experiences in the British Countryside

The British countryside offers a unique culinary experience, with fresh local produce and traditional dishes prepared with high quality ingredients. Culinary tours in the Cotswolds, for example, allow you to visit local farms, dairies and bakeries, sampling artisan produce such as cheeses, breads and pastries. Many of these tours also include gourmet lunches in historic inns, where you can sample dishes prepared with seasonal and local ingredients.

In addition, Cornish tours offer the opportunity to sample the famous Cornish pasty, a traditional meat pie, and to visit fish markets where you can buy, and taste freshly caught seafood.

5. Craft Beer Tasting

The UK has a long brewing tradition, and the craft beer scene is booming. Craft beer tastings offer the opportunity to discover a wide range of beer styles, from classic ales and stouts to more innovative and experimental beers. The cities of Manchester and Bristol are renowned for their craft breweries, with numerous tours including brewery visits, meetings with brewers and guided tastings.

Gourmet experiences in the UK offer a sensory journey through flavors, traditions and culinary innovations. From London food tours to whisky tastings in Scotland, from English vineyards to craft breweries, each experience is an opportunity to discover the richness of British cuisine. Whether you are a food enthusiast, wine lover or whisky connoisseur, the UK's gourmet experiences promise to delight and surprise, creating unforgettable memories.

Adventure Travel: Safari and Exploration in the UK

The UK is known for its history, culture and breathtaking landscapes, but it is also an ideal destination for adventure lovers. From wilderness safaris to explorations of natural wonders, the UK offers a wide range of adventurous activities that promise unique thrills and discoveries. This text will explore some of the best opportunities for adventure travelers in the UK, with a particular focus on safaris and explorations that allow you to immerse yourself in nature and enjoy unforgettable experiences.

Safaris in the UK

When people think of safaris, the plains of Africa probably come to mind, but the UK offers its own versions of safaris, allowing visitors to observe local wildlife in natural settings.

1. Highland Wildlife Safari

In the Scottish Highlands, it is possible to go on a Highland Wildlife Safari. These guided safaris offer the opportunity to see some of Scotland's most iconic species, including red deer, golden eagles, otters and, with any luck, the rare Scottish wildcat. Safaris can be done in 4x4 vehicles or on foot, accompanied by expert guides who share fascinating information about the local flora and fauna.

2. Pembrokeshire Coast National Park

The Pembrokeshire Coast National Park in Wales offers marine safaris that are perfect for observing the UK's marine wildlife. During a boat safari, you can spot dolphins, grey seals and a variety of seabirds. The waters around the islands of Skomer and Ramsey are particularly rich in marine life, and guided excursions offer a unique perspective on the biodiversity of the area.

Explorations in the UK

In addition to safaris, the UK is full of opportunities for adventurous explorations that allow you to discover spectacular landscapes and hidden corners of the country.

1. Cave Exploration in the Peak District

The Peak District is famous for its limestone caves, which offer an underground adventure for brave explorers. Castleton's cave system includes attractions such as Speedwell Cavern, where visitors can take a boat tour through a flooded cave, and Peak Cavern, known as the 'Devil's Cavern'. These caves offer a fascinating insight into the geological formations and mining history of the region.

2. Coastal Walks and Cliff Climbing

The UK's rugged coastline offers plenty of opportunities for adventurous walking and climbing. The Jurassic Coast, a UNESCO World Heritage Site, is an extraordinary place for coastal exploration. Here, you can find fossils of ancient dinosaurs and enjoy breathtaking views. The Cliffs of

Dover are another iconic place for hiking and climbing, offering spectacular views of the English Channel.

3. Kayaking and Canoeing Adventures

The rivers and coastlines of the UK offer excellent opportunities for kayaking and canoeing. The River Wye, which flows through Wales and England, is one of the most popular places for these activities. Kayaking trips along the River Wye allow you to explore picturesque landscapes, see wildlife and, in some stretches, tackle thrilling rapids. For a coastal experience, sea kayaking along the Cornish coast offers explorations of sea caves and hidden bays.

4. Mountain Biking in the Scottish Highlands

The Scottish Highlands are a mountain biker's paradise. With trails through some of Scotland's most spectacular scenery, cyclists can tackle routes ranging from easy scenic trails to expert technical routes. The 7stanes, a series of seven mountain biking centers in the south of Scotland, offer a wide range of trails suitable for all skill levels.

The UK is a surprisingly adventure-packed destination, offering safaris and exploration for every type of traveler. Whether observing wildlife in the Scottish Highlands, exploring the caves of the Peak District, climbing spectacular cliffs or sailing along rivers and coastlines, the opportunities for adventurous experiences are endless. Each adventure offers a unique way to connect with nature and discover the hidden wonders of the UK, making each trip unforgettable.

Chapter 9 Exploring Local Culture

Exploring local culture is one of the most enriching experiences a traveler can have. The UK, with its rich history and cultural diversity, offers endless opportunities to immerse yourself in local traditions, discover the daily lives of the people and better understand the essence of each place you visit. This chapter is dedicated to guiding you through a journey that will take you into the heart of local communities, from bustling cities to quiet villages, and introduce you to the many facets of British culture.

A Mosaic of Traditions and Stories

The United Kingdom is made up of four nations - England, Scotland, Wales and Northern Ireland - each with its own unique cultural identity and traditions. Exploring these diverse local cultures means not only visiting the most famous tourist spots, but also going beyond them, discovering the stories, legends and traditions that make each region special. Whether it's attending a traditional festival, visiting local museums or simply chatting with locals, each experience contributes to a completer and more authentic picture of the UK.

Living Traditions: Festivals and Celebrations

Going to customary festivals and festivities is one of the best methods to learn about the local way of life. There are distinctive events reflecting local history and customs in every corner of the United Kingdom. For example, the Notting Hill Carnival in London is a vibrant celebration of Caribbean culture, while the Edinburgh Festival Fringe is the largest performing arts festival in the world, with shows ranging from comedy to avant-garde theatre. In Wales, the National Eisteddfod celebrates Welsh language and culture with poetry and music competitions, while in Northern Ireland, St. Patrick's Day is a celebration of national pride with parades and traditional music.

Local Gastronomy: A Journey into Flavours

Cuisine is a key aspect of local culture, and each region of the UK has its own gastronomic specialities. Exploring local markets, traditional pubs and neighbourhood restaurants allows you to discover authentic flavors and recipes passed down from generation to generation. From a full Scottish breakfast of haggis and black pudding to traditional English fish and chips, Welsh rarebit and Irish stew, each dish tells a story and offers a taste of the local culture. Participating in food tours or cooking classes can further enrich this experience, allowing you to learn the secrets of local preparations and appreciate the culinary diversity of the UK.

Arts and Crafts: Expressions of Local Culture

Arts and crafts are equally important for understanding local culture. Visiting art galleries, museums and artists' studios offers a glimpse into the creative expressions that characterize each region. From contemporary works by British artists to traditional crafts such as Scottish tweed or Welsh pottery, each piece reflects a part of the local history and culture. Participating in workshops and craft workshops offers the opportunity to create something unique, taking home a tangible piece of the cultural experience.

History and Architecture: Witnesses of the Past

Exploring local culture also means immersing yourself in local history and architecture. The towns and villages of the UK are rich in historic buildings, castles, churches and monuments that tell the story of the past. Walking the streets of York, visiting Edinburgh Castle or exploring the Roman ruins of Bath offers a journey back in time that gives insight into the historical roots of British culture. Guided tours and historical tours are excellent ways to learn more about local history and discover fascinating details that often escape the eyes of hurried tourists.

Exploring local culture in the UK is a journey full of discoveries and surprises. Every experience, from traditional holidays to local cuisine, from art to architecture, contributes to a complete and authentic picture of British life. This chapter will guide you through the many facets of local culture, offering tips and advice on how to fully immerse yourself in the traditions and daily life of the different regions of the UK. Enjoy your cultural journey!

UK Festivals and Cultural Events

The UK is a vibrant crossroads of cultures, traditions and celebrations. Every year, the country hosts a wide range of festivals and cultural events that attract visitors from all over the world. These events not only reflect the diversity and richness of British culture, but also offer unique opportunities to immerse oneself in local traditions, experience new art forms and create unforgettable memories. Below we explore some of the UK's most significant festivals and cultural events.

1. Edinburgh Festival Fringe

The world's largest performing arts festival, the Edinburgh Festival Fringe, takes place every August in the Scottish capital. This extraordinary event hosts thousands of artists presenting theatre, dance, comedy, music and visual arts performances in every corner of the city. The Fringe is known for its inclusive atmosphere and the variety of its performances, which range from traditional to more experimental productions. Attending this festival means an intense and diverse cultural experience, with the opportunity to discover emerging talent and see unique performances.

2. Notting Hill Carnival

The Notting Hill Carnival, held in London every August, is a vibrant celebration of Caribbean culture. Born in the 1960s as a response to racial unrest and social tensions, the carnival has become one of Europe's biggest street festivals. Featuring parades of floats, live music, dancing and Caribbean food, the Notting Hill Carnival attracts millions of visitors and offers a unique experience of cultural integration and collective joy. Reggae, calypso, salsa and soca music creates an electrifying atmosphere, while colorful costumes and energetic performances make this event must-see.

3. Glastonbury Festival

One of the most famous music events in the world takes place in June in Somerset and is called Glastonbury Festival. Glastonbury was founded in 1970 and has played host to some of the biggest names in music, including

Beyoncé and the Rolling Stones. But it is not just music that makes this festival special: Glastonbury is also a major cultural event that includes theatre, dance, poetry, visual arts and much more. Its bohemian atmosphere and commitment to sustainability and social causes make Glastonbury a unique event that goes beyond just a concert to offer a complete cultural experience.

4. Hay Festival

The Hay Festival, held in the picturesque town of Hay-on-Wye in Wales, is a world-renowned literary festival. Every May, writers, thinkers and readers come together to celebrate literature and ideas. With a packed programme of talks, debates, readings and workshops, the Hay Festival offers a unique opportunity to meet celebrated authors, discover new talent and participate in stimulating discussions on a wide range of topics. The relaxed and welcoming atmosphere of the city, known as the 'city of books', contributes to making this event a true paradise for literature lovers.

5. Edinburgh International Book Festival

Also in Edinburgh, but in August, is the Edinburgh International Book Festival, one of the most prestigious literary events in the world. Hosted in Charlotte Square Gardens, the festival attracts authors, publishers and readers from all over the globe. With a programme that includes book presentations, interviews, discussions and workshops, the festival is an opportunity to explore the world of contemporary literature and meet your favorite authors. The cozy atmosphere and direct interaction with authors make this event a unique experience for every book lover.

6. Hogmanay

Hogmanay is the famous Scottish New Year, with the main celebrations taking place in Edinburgh. This event starts on 31 December and continues for three days, with a mix of ancient traditions and modern celebrations. Highlights include the Torchlight Procession, where thousands of people parade with lit torches through the streets of Edinburgh, and the open-air concerts and midnight fireworks that light up the castle. Hogmanay is known for its vibrant energy and warm welcome, making it one of the best ways to celebrate the New Year.

The UK's festivals and cultural events offer an extraordinary insight into the country's diversity and creativity. Each event, with its own peculiarities and traditions, allows you to immerse yourself in the local culture, discover new perspectives and experience unforgettable moments. Whether it is a big music festival, a colorful street parade, a literary event or traditional celebrations, there is always something special to discover and experience in the UK.

Local Markets and Craft Fairs

Craft fairs and local markets are genuine gems of British culture. These events offer not only an extraordinary variety of unique, handmade products, but also a valuable opportunity to discover local traditions, support artisans and immerse yourself in the lively atmosphere of local communities. Below we explore some of the UK's most renowned craft markets and fairs, highlighting what makes them special and why they should be included in your itinerary.

Portobello Road Market, London

One of London's most iconic markets is undoubtedly Portobello Road Market. Located in the Notting Hill district, this market is famous for its antiques section, but also offers a wide range of crafts, fashion, food and more. Every Saturday, the streets fill with stalls selling unique items, from handmade ceramics to fashion accessories made by local designers. To stroll through Portobello Road market is to immerse yourself in a mix of colors, sounds and smells, discovering pieces of art and craft that tell unique stories.

Borough Market, London

Borough Market is a food lover's paradise, but it also offers a selection of high-quality handicrafts. Located near London Bridge, this historic market dates back over 1000 years and is now one of London's leading food markets. In addition to gastronomic delights, you will also find artisans selling products such as pottery, handmade kitchenware and household items. The market is open every day, but Thursdays, Fridays and Saturdays are the best days to visit and enjoy the lively atmosphere and wide selection of products.

Bath Craft Fairs

The city of Bath, famous for its Roman baths and Georgian architecture, hosts several craft fairs throughout the year. The best known is probably the Bath Christmas Market, which takes place over the Christmas period. This festive market transforms the streets of the city center into a Christmas village, with over 150 chalets selling local crafts, Christmas decorations and gourmet food. It is a perfect opportunity to buy unique, handmade gifts while enjoying the city's magical atmosphere during the festive season.

St. Nicholas Market, Bristol

St. Nicholas Market, located in the heart of Bristol, is a historic market dating back to 1743. This covered market is well-known for both its extensive product selection and lively atmosphere. Everything from fine art prints to handcrafted jewellery, vintage clothing to handcrafted accessories, may be found here. The market is open seven days a week, with various special events and themed markets held throughout the year, such as the farmers' market and the Christmas market.

York Craft Fairs

The city of York, with its rich history and picturesque streets, is a great place to explore craft fairs. The York Festival of Crafts, held in summer, is one of the city's main events. This fair brings together artisans from all over the country, offering a wide range of handmade products, including ceramics, textiles, jewellery and artwork. Attending this fair means not only buying unique items, but also meeting the artists and discovering the stories behind their creations.

Grassington Market, Yorkshire Dales

Grassington, a charming village in the heart of the Yorkshire Dales, hosts a craft market that attracts visitors from all over the region. The Grassington Dickensian Festival, held during the Christmas period, is particularly popular. This event transforms the village into a Victorian scene, with stalls selling local crafts, street performances, live music and entertainment for the whole family. It is a unique experience that combines shopping, culture and local traditions.

Local markets and craft fairs in the UK offer an authentic immersion into British culture. Each market and fair have its own unique character, reflecting the traditions and craft skills of the region. Visiting these places is not just about shopping, but also about supporting local artisans, discovering fascinating stories and taking home unique pieces that tell a part of your travel experience. Whether it is a bustling urban market or a craft fare in a picturesque country village, these experiences will enrich your trip to the UK, offering unforgettable and authentic moments.

Theatres, Concerts and Performances

The UK is renowned for its vibrant cultural and arts scene, offering a wide range of theatres, concerts and shows that attract fans from all over the world. From iconic theatre performances to concerts by international artists, the UK is a haven for those who love the performing arts. In this text, we explore some of the most significant venues and events, illustrating what makes them special and unmissable.

Theatre in the UK

West End, London

London's West End is synonymous with quality theatre. Known as the heart of British theatre, it is home to some of the world's most famous musicals and theatre productions. Iconic theatres such as the Royal Opera House, the London Palladium and the Apollo Victoria offer performances ranging from classics like 'Les Misérables' and 'The Phantom of the Opera' to innovative new productions. Every year, millions of visitors flock to the West End to experience the thrill of a live performance in some of the world's most historic and renowned theatres.

Shakespeare's Globe, London

For a unique theatre experience, Shakespeare's Globe is a must. Located on the south bank of the Thames, this theatre is a faithful reconstruction of William Shakespeare's original Globe Theatre. Here, you can see productions that replicate the Elizabethan theatre experience, with outdoor performances and a standing room only audience in the parterre area. The Globe offers a range of Shakespearean and other classic productions, presented in an authentic setting that transports spectators back in time.

Concerts in the UK

Royal Albert Hall, London

Among the world's most esteemed concert halls is the Royal Albert Hall. This magnificent auditorium, which opened in 1871, accommodates a range of events, including pop and rock stars as well as classical music concerts. The annual BBC Proms event is particularly famous, offering a series of classical music concerts during the summer culminating in the spectacular 'Last Night of the Proms'. Every performance at the iconic Royal Albert Hall is enhanced by its superb acoustics and striking architecture.

O2 Arena, London

For fans of contemporary music, the O2 Arena is the ideal venue. Located on the Greenwich Peninsula, the O2 is one of the largest indoor arenas in the world and hosts concerts by international artists, comedy shows and sporting events. With a capacity of over 20,000 spectators, the O2 offers an immersive and vibrant experience with a packed calendar of events spanning a variety of musical genres.

Shows and Festivals in the UK

Edinburgh Festival Fringe

Every August, the capital of Scotland hosts the largest performing arts festival in the world, the Edinburgh Festival Fringe. The Fringe hosts thousands of artists presenting theatre, dance, comedy, music and visual arts performances at various venues around the city. This festival is known for its inclusiveness and variety of performances, ranging from traditional to more experimental productions. Attending the Fringe means immersing yourself in a creative and dynamic atmosphere, discovering emerging talent and witnessing unique performances.

Glastonbury Festival

One of the most famous music events in the world takes place in June in Somerset and is called Glastonbury Festival. Glastonbury was founded in 1970 and has played host to some of the biggest names in music, including Beyoncé and the Rolling Stones. But it is not just music that makes this festival special: Glastonbury is also a major cultural event that includes theatre, dance, poetry, visual arts and much more. Its bohemian atmosphere and commitment to sustainability and social causes make Glastonbury a unique event that goes beyond just a concert to offer a complete cultural experience.

The UK offers an unrivalled cultural and arts scene, with a wide range of theatres, concerts and shows to suit all tastes. Whether attending a musical in the West End, enjoying a concert at the Royal Albert Hall, attending a festival such as the Edinburgh Festival Fringe or exploring new talent at Glastonbury, there is always something exciting to discover. These events not only enrich the cultural life of the country, but also offer unforgettable experiences to everyone who visits them.

Discovering Local Cuisine: Cookery Courses and Gastronomic Tours

The United Kingdom, with its rich history and cultural diversity, offers a vibrant and ever-changing culinary scene. Discovering local cuisine through cookery courses and food tours is an excellent way to immerse yourself in British culinary traditions, learn new skills and enjoy authentic dishes. In this text we explore the benefits and opportunities offered by these gastronomic experiences, highlighting some of the best options available in the UK.

Cookery Courses: Learning from the Roots

Leiths Cookery School, London

Leiths Cooking School in London is one of the most prestigious culinary institutions in the UK. It offers a wide range of courses, from long-term professional programmes to one-day workshops for cooking enthusiasts of all levels. Taking a cookery course at Leiths allows you to learn fundamental cooking techniques, explore traditional and contemporary British cuisine, and prepare dishes under the guidance of experienced chefs.

River Cottage, Devon

River Cottage, founded by celebrity chef Hugh Fearnley-Whittingstall, is situated in the beautiful Devon countryside. Here, participants can take courses ranging from baking to butchery, from horticulture to sustainable cooking. Courses are designed to teach not only how to prepare delicious dishes, but also how to choose fresh, local ingredients, promoting ethical and sustainable cooking.

The Raymond Blanc Cookery School, Oxfordshire

Located at the famous Belmond Le Manoir aux Quat'Saisons restaurant and hotel, The Raymond Blanc Cookery School offers a luxurious culinary experience. Taught by highly qualified chefs, the courses cover a wide range of topics, from classic French cuisine to the preparation of modern British dishes. Each course is designed to inspire and enhance participants' culinary skills, offering a unique opportunity to learn in a refined and stimulating environment.

Food Tours: A Journey in Taste

London Food Tours

London, with its incredible culinary variety, is the ideal place for a food tour. Several companies offer walking tours that explore neighbourhoods famous for their culinary offerings, such as Borough Market, Soho and Shoreditch. These guided tours allow you to sample local specialities, visit historic markets and discover hidden restaurants, offering a comprehensive overview of London's culinary traditions and trends.

The Cotswolds Food and Drink Experience

The Cotswolds, with its picturesque villages and lush countryside, offers a unique gastronomic experience. Food tours in the region include visits to local cheese makers, craft breweries, oil mills and farmhouses. These tours allow you to sample fresh, high-quality produce directly from the producers, offering total immersion in local culinary traditions.

Edinburgh Food Safari

Edinburgh, with its rich history and vibrant culinary scene, is another perfect destination for a food tour. The Edinburgh Food Safari takes participants through the city's best restaurants, cafes and markets. Visitors can savor traditional Scottish dishes such as haggis, taste aged malt whisky and discover local sweets such as Scottish tablet. This tour offers a comprehensive overview of Edinburgh's culinary delights, combined with interesting anecdotes about the city's history and culture.

The Benefits of Culinary Experiences

Participating in cooking classes and culinary tours offers numerous benefits. Not only do you acquire new culinary skills and deepen your knowledge of local ingredients, but you also have the opportunity to socialize with people who share the same passion for cooking. These experiences are ideal for couples, friends and families, creating unforgettable memories while exploring new culinary cultures.

In addition, learning to cook traditional dishes and discovering local products helps support the local economy and promotes sustainable food practices. Local chefs and guides often share valuable tips on how to choose fresh, seasonal ingredients, encouraging a healthier, more conscious lifestyle.

Discovering local cuisine through cooking classes and food tours is a great way to immerse yourself in British culture, learn new skills and savor unique culinary delights. Whether taking a course at a renowned cookery school or joining a food tour in a historic city, these experiences offer the perfect mix of learning, fun and discovery. The UK, with its rich culinary tradition and constant innovation, is the ideal destination for anyone wishing to explore the world through food.

Attend traditional celebrations such as Guy Fawkes Night and the Notting Hill Carnival

The UK is famous for its vibrant and colorful traditional celebrations, which offer a unique opportunity to immerse yourself in the local culture and experience historical and festive events. Two of the most emblematic celebrations are Guy Fawkes Night and the Notting Hill Carnival. These events offer not only entertainment and festivities, but also an immersion in British traditions and history. In this text, we will explore each of these celebrations in detail, highlighting their importance and how to participate in them for an authentic and memorable experience.

Guy Fawkes Night: A Historical Celebration

Every year on November 5th, Guy Fawkes Night, sometimes referred to as Bonfire Night, is celebrated. This celebration commemorates the failed attack on the House of Lords by Guy Fawkes and his accomplices in 1605, known as the Bonfire Conspiracy. Fawkes' aim was to blow up Parliament and assassinate King James I, but the plan was foiled, and the conspirators were arrested and convicted.

Today, Guy Fawkes Night is celebrated throughout the UK with spectacular bonfires and fireworks. The celebrations begin on the evening of 5 November and include a series of traditional events. Families and communities gather to light bonfires, which are often accompanied by the traditional Guy Fawkes figure, a straw and rag representation that is burnt as a symbol of the conspirators' condemnation.

Participation and Celebrations

Bonfires and Fireworks: Participating in a public bonfire is one of the best ways to experience Guy Fawkes Night. Towns and villages all over the UK organize events with spectacular fireworks and large bonfires. Some of the best-known places to celebrate include Battersea Park in London and Llandudno rugby ground in Wales.

Food and Traditions: During the celebration, it is common to enjoy typical specialities such as 'toffee apples' (caramelized apples), 'parkins' (a kind of cake made of oats and molasses) and 'bangers' (sausages). These traditional foods are often found at local market stalls and are a delicious way to immerse yourself in British gastronomic culture.

Local Events: Many municipalities organize events and shows centred around the story of Guy Fawkes. Attending one of the many historical re-enactments or a public reading of the Conjuring of the Powers can offer a deeper understanding of the historical importance of this celebration.

Notting Hill Carnival: An Explosion of Culture and Color

The Notting Hill Carnival is one of Europe's largest and most famous street festivals, held annually in London during the Bank Holiday weekend in August. Originating in the 1960s as a celebration of Caribbean and Afro-British culture, the carnival has grown into an event that embraces a wide range of cultures and communities, representing a vibrant celebration of diversity and inclusion.

Participation and Celebration

Parades and Music: The heart of the Notting Hill Carnival is its colorful and lively parade. The streets of the Notting Hill district are filled with decorated floats, groups of dancers in elaborate costumes and bands playing calypso and soca music. Participating in the parade allows you to experience the energy and excitement of the carnival, as participants join in the addictive rhythm of the music.

Food and Markets: The carnival offers an extraordinary variety of food from around the world, with stalls serving Caribbean dishes such as jerk chicken, patties and plantains. Exploring the food markets during the festival is an unmissable opportunity to sample authentic dishes and discover new cuisines.

Events and Shows: In addition to the main parade, the Notting Hill Carnival presents a range of cultural events, including dances, art performances and workshops. Visitors can watch dance performances, participate in costume workshops and enjoy live performances that reflect London's rich cultural diversity.

Participating in traditional celebrations such as Guy Fawkes Night and the Notting Hill Carnival offers a unique insight into British traditions and culture. These events not only provide extraordinary entertainment, but also an opportunity to better understand the history and diversity of the United Kingdom. Whether watching spectacular fireworks or dancing to Caribbean music, these celebrations offer unforgettable experiences that will enrich your trip and your understanding of Britain's rich cultural heritage.

Visits to historic breweries and distilleries with tastings of local products

The UK is renowned for its long tradition of brewing and distilling, with historic breweries and distilleries offering a fascinating foray into the world of craft spirits. Visiting these places not only allows you to discover the history and culture of these iconic beverages, but also to taste high-quality local products through guided tastings. In this text, we explore some of the UK's most celebrated historic breweries and distilleries and the unique experiences they offer.

Historic Breweries

Fuller's Brewery, London

Fuller's Brewery, located in Chiswick, London, is one of the oldest and most respected breweries in the UK. Founded in 1845, Fuller's is famous for its traditional beers such as London Pride and ESB. A visit to the brewery includes a guided tour of the historic facilities, where you can see traditional and modern brewing methods. During the tour, guests can learn about the history of beer and brewing, from ingredient selection to fermentation. The tour ends with a beer tasting, accompanied by detailed explanations of the different styles and flavors.

The Beavertown Brewery, London

Located in Tottenham, the Beavertown Brewery is known for its innovative and high-quality craft beers. Founded in 2011, Beavertown has quickly gained popularity for its bold and tasty beers. The brewery tour includes a walk through the brewing process, from wort preparation to final packaging. Guests can enjoy a selection of fresh beers straight from the source, discovering how innovative recipes and techniques help create unique taste experiences.

BrewDog, Aberdeenshire

BrewDog is another example of a brewery that has revolutionized the craft beer landscape. Founded in Ellon, Aberdeenshire, in 2007, BrewDog has become renowned for its bold beers and innovative approach. A visit to the brewery includes a walk through the modern production facilities and a tasting of beers, including some of their iconic products such as Punk IPA and Elvis Juice. Visitors also have the opportunity to learn from the BrewDog team and discover the secrets behind their brewing philosophy.

Historic Distilleries

The Glenlivet Distillery, Moray

The Glenlivet Distillery, located in the Speyside region, is one of the UK's most historic and respected whisky distilleries. Founded in 1824, Glenlivet is famous for its single malt whisky. A visit to the distillery includes a tour that explores the history of whisky production and the traditional techniques used to create their renowned single malt. Visitors can sample a selection of Glenlivet whiskies, with detailed explanations on how each expression differs in terms of taste and aroma.

The Macallan Distillery, Moray

The Macallan Distillery, located in the Speyside region, is also a landmark for whisky lovers. Founded in 1824, Macallan is known for its high-quality single malts, often aged in sherry casks. The visit includes a tour of the modern production facilities and historic cellars. Guests have the opportunity to taste a selection of Macallan single malts, with an expert guide explaining the ageing process and the unique characteristics of each whisky.

Hendrick's Gin Distillery, Girvan

For gin aficionados, Hendrick's Gin Distillery is a must-visit destination. Located in Girvan, Ayrshire, Hendrick's is famous for its unique gin, flavored with cucumber and rose petals. A visit to the distillery offers a fascinating tour that explores Hendrick's history and production philosophy. During the visit, you can see the distinctive stills and taste the gin through a guided tasting session, discovering how the botanical ingredients contribute to its distinctive flavor.

Visits to historic breweries and distilleries offer a fascinating insight into the world of spirits production, allowing you to discover the history and traditions that have shaped the UK's food scene. Through guided tours and tastings of local products, you can appreciate the quality and variety of British beers and spirits, while gaining in-depth knowledge of production processes and craft techniques. Whether exploring a historic brewery in London or tasting a world-renowned whisky in Speyside, these experiences offer a unique opportunity to discover and appreciate the beverages that have helped define British food culture.

Chapter 10 Time Management and Emotional Well-being

Retirement represents a chapter in life full of new opportunities and challenges. After years of work and daily routine, the transition to retirement can be both liberating and disorienting. On the one hand, there is the chance to pursue passions never before explored and to enjoy unprecedented freedom. On the other, however, there can be anxiety about readjusting to a new routine and managing free time. For many, this change involves not only a restructuring of the day, but also an opportunity for personal growth and finding a new emotional balance.

Managing time in retirement becomes crucial to ensure lasting well-being. Without the structures imposed by work, it is easy to feel lost or overwhelmed by an infinity of options and new freedoms. That is why conscious time planning can make the difference between a retirement full of satisfaction and a life of boredom and disorientation. Creating a routine that balances stimulating activities, moments of relaxation and opportunities for socializing is crucial to maintaining a good state of mind and making the most of this phase of life.

Practical time management is not more significant than emotional well-being. Retirement can bring with it a wide range of emotions, from joy and freedom to a possible loss of identity and a feeling of isolation. Coping with these emotional changes requires a careful awareness of one's needs and a proactive approach to self-care. Participating in new activities, establishing new social connections, and maintaining a positive mindset are key to successfully navigating this transition.

In this chapter, we will explore effective strategies for time management and emotional well-being in retirement. We will explore how to create a routine that integrates rewarding and stimulating activities, and how to identify and address emotional challenges that may arise. In addition, we will discuss the importance of setting realistic and meaningful goals that can contribute to a sense of purpose and fulfilment.

Retirement provides the chance to start afresh and explore new hobbies and passions. With careful planning and a positive approach, it is possible to turn this period of change into a rewarding and enriching adventure. Through effective time management techniques and practices for emotional well-being, you can approach retirement with confidence and joy, fully enjoying the new freedoms and opportunities it brings.

Balancing Activity and Rest

Retirement represents a stage in life when you finally have time to pursue the passions and interests you neglected during your working years. However, with this new freedom also comes the need to find a balance between activity and rest. Balancing these two aspects is crucial to maintaining a healthy and fulfilling life, avoiding the risk of burnout or a monotonous routine. This text will explore the importance of a balance between activity and rest and provide practical tips for achieving and maintaining this harmony in retirement life.

The Importance of Balance

Physical and mental well-being depend on a healthy balance between activity and rest. While stimulating and rewarding activities can keep the mind active and the body fit, rest is essential to regain energy and prevent stress. Excessive activity without adequate breaks can lead to fatigue and irritability, while too much time spent without stimulation can cause boredom and feelings of worthlessness.

Strategies for Balancing Activity and Rest

1. Create a Weekly Routine

A well-planned routine can help balance activities and rest periods. Consider planning your weeks with a mix of commitments and free time. For example, you can set aside specific days for social activities, hobbies, exercise and time for yourself. Including regular rest periods in your routine, such as relaxing reading or leisurely walks, can help you avoid overload.

2. Set Realistic Goals

Maintaining a healthy balance requires setting goals that are both reachable and practical. Goals should be motivating but not overly demanding. If you enjoy trekking, for instance, schedule short walks and progressively extend the distance. Similarly, if you have a hobby that requires concentration, make sure you take regular breaks to avoid mental fatigue.

3. Incorporate Relaxation Moments

Rest is not just a break from work, but an opportunity to rejuvenate. Integrate relaxing activities such as meditation, yoga or simple walks in the green into your routine. These peaceful times aid in lowering stress and enhancing overall wellbeing. Taking time for simple everyday pleasures, such as listening to music or reading a book, can make a big difference in maintaining a healthy balance.

4. Listening to Your Body and Mind

Being aware of the signals of your body and mind is essential for managing the balance between activity and rest. Give yourself time to recuperate if you're feeling drained or anxious. On the other hand, if you feel lethargic or underused, it may be time to introduce new activities or challenges. Keeping honest communication with yourself will help you find and maintain the right balance.

5. Participate in Social Activities and Stay Active

Sustaining a vibrant social life is crucial for mental health. Participating in interest groups or community events can provide mental stimulation and socializing opportunities, contributing to a richer and more varied life. But it's also important to exercise caution so that you don't take on too many social obligations. Strike a balance so that you can socialise with others without sacrificing your alone or free time.

6. Do Regular Physical Activity

Exercise is a key element in maintaining good health and a balance between activity and rest. Select enjoyable and health-promoting hobbies for yourself, like yoga, swimming, or strolling. Regular physical activity not only improves your physical condition, but also contributes to better sleep and a more relaxed mind.

Maintaining a healthy and meaningful life in retirement requires striking a balance between work and play. Creating a balanced routine, setting realistic goals, and listening to one's physical and mental needs are crucial steps in achieving this balance. With conscious planning and a balanced approach, it is possible to fully enjoy the opportunities offered by retirement, maintaining a lasting well-being and a fulfilling life.

Maintaining Social and Family Relationships

Retirement marks a new phase in life, when time and opportunities for socializing and maintaining relationships expand. However, this transitional period can also bring challenges in maintaining and nurturing social and family ties. As daily routines change and habitual contacts may be lost, it is crucial to devote attention and effort to preserving and enriching these relationships. This text will explore how to maintain and enhance social and family relationships in retirement, and the importance of these connections for overall well-being.

The Importance of Social and Family Relationships

Social and family relationships have a significant impact on emotional and psychological well-being. Staying connected with family and friends helps prevent feelings of isolation and loneliness, which can be common during retirement. Social interactions foster a sense of belonging and support and can improve quality of life through exchanges of experiences and mutual support. In addition, having an active social network can contribute to maintaining a positive mindset and good mental health.

Strategies for Maintaining and Strengthening Relationships

1. Plan Regular Meetings

Establishing regular meetings with family and friends is essential for maintaining close ties. Organizing lunches, dinners or simple weekly or monthly meetings helps to keep the connection alive. These meetings do not always have to be in person; video calls or phone calls can also be a great way to stay in touch, especially if family members or friends live far away.

2. Participate in Group Activities

Joining groups or clubs with common interests can offer excellent opportunities to make new acquaintances and expand your social network. Participating in courses, volunteer activities, or community events allows you to meet people with similar passions, facilitating the creation of new friendships. These activities not only enrich social life, but also provide mental and physical stimulation.

3. Keep Communication Active

Being proactive in communication is key to maintaining strong relationships. Don't wait for others to make the first move; send messages, make phone calls and show interest in the lives of others. Sharing updates about your own life and listening to others' stories creates an ongoing dialogue and strengthens the bond.

4. Celebrate Special Occasions

Celebrations and special occasions, such as birthdays, anniversaries and holidays, are ideal times to strengthen relationships. Plan and attend family and social parties or events, and make your loved ones feel how important they are. These moments of sharing and celebration are invaluable for maintaining bonds and creating meaningful memories.

5. Be Available and Supportive

Being a good friend or family member also means being available and ready to offer support when needed. Be present during difficult times and offer practical or emotional help. Being willing to support others in times of need not only strengthens relationships, but also helps build an environment of mutual support and trust.

6. Invest in New Encounters

Retirement is a great opportunity to expand your social circle and meet new people. Attend events, courses or activities that allow you to meet new people. Being open to new connections and friendships enriches life and can lead to lasting and satisfying relationships.

Facing Challenges

Retirement can bring challenges such as changing family roles or losing regular contacts. Facing these challenges requires flexibility and adaptation. Accept that relationships may evolve and try to keep a positive mindset about the changes. If necessary, seek support from a counsellor or support groups to deal with any relationship difficulties.

Maintaining and enhancing social and family relationships in retirement is essential for emotional well-being and quality of life. Planning regular meetings, participating in group activities, and maintaining active communication are key strategies for preserving meaningful bonds. Being proactive in building and maintaining relationships not only prevents isolation, but also enriches life with new experiences and valuable connections. With commitment and focus, it is possible to fully enjoy social and family relationships in retirement, creating an enriching network of support and affection every day.

Mindfulness and Relaxation Techniques

Retirement represents a stage of life in which time and opportunities for personal reflection and improved emotional well-being are expanded. In this context, mindfulness and relaxation techniques emerge as key tools for maintaining a peaceful mind and emotional balance. These practices not only help manage stress and anxiety, but also promote greater awareness and satisfaction in daily life. This text will explore mindfulness and relaxation techniques, offering practical guidance on how to integrate them into daily routines.

Mindfulness: Being Present in the Moment

Mindfulness, or mindfulness, is the practice of focusing fully on the present moment, accepting experiences, thoughts and emotions without judgement. This practice can significantly reduce stress and improve overall well-being.

1. Mindfulness meditation

Mindfulness meditation is a key technique that involves concentrating on a specific aspect of the present moment, such as the breath. To begin, find a quiet place, sit comfortably and close your eyes. Pay attention to your breathing and note when you inhale and exhale. When your thoughts stray, acknowledge them without passing judgement on them and gently return your focus to the breath. Even ten to fifteen minute daily workouts might have a significant impact.

2. Body scan

A mindfulness exercise called the "body scan" involves concentrating attention on various bodily areas and observing any tension or relaxation or sensations. Shut your eyes while you sit or lie down in a comfortable position. Focus first on your feet, then gradually raise your gaze to your head. This exercise facilitates the release of stored stress and increases awareness of physical sensations.

3. Mindfulness in Daily Activities

Including mindfulness in regular tasks is a good method to develop awareness. During activities such as eating, walking or showering, pay attention to sensory details and sensations. For example, while eating, focus on tastes, textures and the act of chewing, rather than distracting yourself with the television or phone.

Relaxation Techniques: Promoting Serenity

Relaxation techniques help reduce stress levels and promote a state of calm and tranquility. These techniques are especially helpful for people who are attempting to control their anxiety and get better sleep.

1. Deep Breathing

One easy yet powerful method for promoting calm is deep breathing. Once you're in a comfortable position, shut your eyes. Count to four as you gently inhale with your nose, and then count to six as you exhale through your mouth. Pay attention to how air feels going in and out of your lungs. This method aids in lowering tension and calming the nervous system.

2. Progressive Muscle Relaxation

In order to reduce stress and tension, progressive muscle relaxation is a technique that involves contracting and relaxing muscles. Choose a comfortable position to sit or lie down. Start with the muscles in your feet, contract and then relax. Slowly work your way upwards through your legs, abdomen, arms and face. This method encourages deep relaxation and raises awareness of tense muscles.

3. Guided Visualization

Guided visualization involves imagining calm and relaxing scenarios to reduce stress. Find a quiet place, close your eyes and imagine a serene place, such as a beach or forest. Pay attention to the specifics of the imagined setting, including the sounds, scents, and feelings. This practice helps to take your mind off everyday worries and promote a state of calm.

Benefits of Mindfulness and Relaxation

The integration of mindfulness and relaxation techniques into daily life offers numerous benefits. These include reduced stress, better emotional management, improved sleep and increased self-awareness. In addition, regularly practicing mindfulness and relaxation can contribute to a more balanced and satisfying life, improving the quality of relationships and the ability to cope with daily challenges.

In retirement, mindfulness and relaxation practices can be effective tools for enhancing mental and emotional health. More balance and tranquilly can be attained by incorporating techniques like progressive muscular relaxation, deep breathing, and mindfulness meditation into everyday routines. With dedication and practice, these techniques can contribute to a more fulfilling and peaceful life, enriching each day with a sense of calm and awareness.

Solving Common Problems: Loneliness and Mental Health

Retirement is a stage of life that offers new freedoms and opportunities, but it can also present significant challenges, including loneliness and mental health problems. These issues can significantly lower quality of life and are prevalent among retirees. Living a happy and meaningful retirement requires addressing loneliness and fostering mental wellness. This text will explore common problems related to loneliness and mental health in old age and provide concrete strategies to deal with them.

Loneliness in old age

Loneliness is a major problem among older people and can result from various factors, such as loss of friends or family, retirement, or reduced social opportunities. This sense of isolation can have a negative impact on mental and physical health, contributing to feelings of sadness, anxiety and depression.

Strategies to Combat Loneliness

1. Maintain and Build Social Connections

An effective way to combat loneliness is to maintain and build social connections. Participating in interest groups, local clubs, or community activities can provide opportunities to meet new people and make new friends. Activities such as art classes, reading groups, or garden clubs not only help pass the time but also connect with others who share similar interests.

2. Volunteering and Group Activities

Volunteering is a great way to stay active and connected to the community. Offering your time to local organizations not only provides a sense of purpose, but also offers opportunities to meet other people and develop new relationships. Group activities, such as fitness classes or walking groups, can also promote regular social interactions and build a support network.

3. Using Technology to Stay Connected

Utilising technology to lessen loneliness can be quite effective. Social media and video calls make it easier to stay in touch with faraway family and friends. Learning to use technology tools, such as Skype or Zoom, can facilitate communication and reduce feelings of isolation.

Mental health in old age

Mental health is just as important as physical health, and problems such as anxiety, depression and stress can be common during retirement. It is essential to recognize these problems and seek support when needed.

Strategies to Improve Mental Health

1. Establish a Routine and Goals

Having a daily routine and clear goals can give a sense of structure and purpose to life. Establishing daily and weekly activities, such as exercise, hobbies and time for personal reflection, helps to keep the mind occupied and reduce the risk of feelings of worthlessness or depression.

2. Seek professional support

Seeking assistance from a mental health expert is crucial if you exhibit signs of anxiety or despair. Therapists and counsellors can offer strategies and techniques for coping and managing mental health problems. Seeking assistance when needed is crucial for achieving emotional well-being; don't put it off.

3. Practicing Relaxation and Mindfulness Techniques

Stress management and mental health can be enhanced by practicing mindfulness and relaxation practices. Deep breathing, progressive muscle relaxation, and meditation are among practices that help lower anxiety and foster peace and tranquilly.

4. Maintain an Active Lifestyle

Mental wellness requires regular physical activity. Even mild activity, like taking regular walks, can lift your spirits and lessen the signs of sadness and anxiety. Endorphins are produced when you exercise, and they are believed to enhance emotional health.

Coping with loneliness and maintaining good mental health are crucial aspects of living a healthy and fulfilling retirement. Creating and sustaining social networks, taking part in group activities, and staying connected via technology can all help fight loneliness. At the same time, establishing a routine, seeking professional support, and practicing relaxation techniques can significantly improve mental health. With a proactive and mindful approach, it is possible to tackle these common problems and enjoy a fulfilling and healthy retirement life.

Conclusion: Embracing an Active and Satisfying Retirement

The journey through retirement is a transitional phase that, if approached with the right mindset and preparation, can turn into a period of great satisfaction and fulfilment. The pages of this book have explored a variety of opportunities and strategies to make life in retirement not only vibrant but also deeply rewarding. We have discussed how to explore new interests, maintain optimal health, and cultivate a meaningful connection to the community and the world around us. In this conclusion, we will reflect on the key points and offer some final thoughts on how to embrace and optimize this new phase of life.

Reflections on the Themes Explored

Physical Activity and Well-being

We have seen how crucial physical activity is to maintaining good health in retirement. Whether it is walks in the woods, participation in sports such as golf, or involvement in water activities, the important thing is to find a balance between exercise and rest. Exploring the various sports and wellness options shows that it is possible to find activities to suit every level of fitness and interest, thus ensuring an improvement in quality of life and a reduction in the risks associated with inactivity.

Volunteering opportunities

Volunteering emerges as a valuable opportunity to remain active and engaged in the community. Involvement in hospitals, retirement homes, and environmental projects not only provides a sense of purpose and personal satisfaction, but also helps build and maintain meaningful social relationships. Volunteering, therefore, is not only an act of service to others, but also a way to enrich one's life and maintain a support network.

Continuous Learning

Continuous learning proves to be a fundamental pillar for stimulating the mind and enriching life. Online courses, senior citizen universities, reading clubs and genealogy studies provide opportunities to explore new knowledge and hobbies. Participating in language or music courses not only stimulates the mind but also offers new avenues for social interaction and fun.

Social and Group Activities

The importance of participating in social and group activities, such as local events, fairs, and clubs, is evident in fostering a sense of belonging and community. These activities not only provide fun and entertainment, but also contribute to strengthening social bonds and improving emotional well-being.

Unique Trips and Experiences

Luxury travel and unique experiences, such as cruises, stays in historic hotels and gastronomic tours, offer the chance to experience memorable and enriching adventures. Planning such experiences not only stimulates curiosity and excitement, but also contributes to a more varied and fulfilling life.

Time Management and Emotional Well-being

Finally, time management and maintaining emotional well-being are essential to living a happy and healthy retirement. Balancing activity and rest, maintaining social and family relationships, and using mindfulness and relaxation techniques are key strategies for managing stress and promoting emotional balance.

Final considerations

In conclusion, retirement is not an end, but rather a beginning of a new phase full of possibilities. By taking a proactive and conscious approach, it is possible to turn this period of life into an opportunity to explore new passions, maintain good health, and build meaningful relationships. It is a time to celebrate the freedom you have gained and to approach life with an open mind and an enthusiastic heart. Whether you are exploring new activities, contributing to the community, or simply enjoying the wonders of everyday life, remember that the journey to a fulfilling retirement is a continuous discovery of self and the world around us. Embrace this phase with curiosity and joy, and let each day bring new opportunities for growth and happiness.

Scan the QR code to receive Your Gift

Printed in Great Britain
by Amazon